# Fabulous Food

Pam Schiller

Special Needs Adaptations by Clarissa Willis

# Acknowledgments

I would like to thank the following people for their contributions to this book. The special needs adaptations were written by Clarissa Willis. The CD is arranged by Patrick

Clarissa Willis     Patrick Brennan     Richele Bartkowiak

Brennan, and performed by Richele Bartkowiak and Patrick Brennan. It is engineered and mixed by Jeff Smith at Southwest Recordings. —Pam Schiller

# Books written by Pam Schiller

*The Bilingual Book of Rhymes, Songs, Stories, and Fingerplays,* with Rafael Lara-Alecio and Beverly J. Irby

*The Complete Book of Activities, Games, Stories, Props, Recipes, and Dances,* with Jackie Silberg

*The Complete Book of Rhymes, Songs, Poems, Fingerplays, and Chants,* with Jackie Silberg

*The Complete Daily Curriculum for Early Childhood: Over 1200 Easy Activities to Support Multiple Intelligences and Learning Styles,* with Pat Phipps

*The Complete Resource Book: An Early Childhood Curriculum,* with Kay Hastings

*The Complete Resource Book for Infants: Over 700 Experiences for Children From Birth to 18 Months*

*The Complete Resource Book for Toddlers and Twos: Over 2000 Experiences and Ideas*

*Count on Math: Activities for Small Hands and Lively Minds,* with Lynne Peterson

*Creating Readers: Over 1000 Games, Activities, Tongue Twisters, Fingerplays, Songs, and Stories to Get Children Excited About Reading*

*Do You Know the Muffin Man?,* with Thomas Moore

*The Instant Curriculum, Revised,* with Joan Rosanno

*The Practical Guide to Quality Child Care,* with Patricia Carter Dyke

*Start Smart: Building Brain Power in the Early Years*

*The Values Book,* with Tamera Bryant

*Where Is Thumbkin?,* with Thomas Moore

# Fabulous Food

## 25 Songs and Over 300 Activities for Young Children

**CD INSIDE!**

**Pam Schiller**

**Gryphon House, Inc.**
**Beltsville, Maryland**

○ spatial organization
○ language, receptive and expressive
○ fine motor coordination
○ cognitive challenges

The following general strategies from Kathleen Bulloch (2003) are for children who have difficulty listening and speaking.

| Difficulty | Adaptations/Modifications/Strategies |
|---|---|
| Listening | ○ Stating the objective—providing a reason for listening<br>○ Using a photo card<br>○ Giving explanations in small, discrete steps<br>○ Being concise with verbal information: "Evan, please sit," instead of "Evan, would you please sit down in your chair?"<br>○ Providing visuals<br>○ Having the child repeat directions<br>○ Having the child close his eyes and try to visualize the information<br>○ Providing manipulative tasks<br>○ When giving directions to the class, leaving a pause between each step so the child can carry out the process in her mind<br>○ Shortening the listening time required<br>○ Pre-teaching difficult vocabulary and concepts |
| Verbal Expression | ○ Providing a prompt, such as beginning the sentence for the child or giving a picture cue<br>○ Accepting an alternate form of information—sharing, such as artistic creation, photos, charade or pantomime, and demonstration<br>○ Asking questions that require short answers<br>○ Specifically teaching body and language expression<br>○ First asking questions at the information level—giving facts and asking for facts back<br>○ Waiting for children to respond; not calling on the first child who raises his hand<br>○ Having the child break in gradually by speaking in smaller groups and then in larger groups |

### English Language Learners

Strategies for English language learners are also provided. These strategies maximize the learning potential for English language learners while providing opportunities for building language concepts.

The following are general strategies for working with English language learners (Gray, Fleischman, 2004-05):

○ Keep the language simple. Speak simply and clearly. Use short, complete sentences in a normal tone of voice. Avoid using slang, idioms, or figures of speech.

○ Use actions and illustrations to reinforce oral statements. Appropriate prompts and facial expressions help convey meaning.

○ Ask for completion, not generation. Ask children to choose answers from a list or to complete a partially finished sentence. Encourage children to use language as much as possible to gain confidence over time.

○ Model correct usage and judiciously correct errors. Use corrections to positively reinforce children's use of English. When English language learners make a mistake or use awkward language, they are often attempting to apply what they know about their first language to English. For example, a Spanish-speaking child may say, "It fell from me," a direct translation from Spanish, instead of "I dropped it."

○ Use visual aids. Present classroom content and information in a way that engages children—by using graphic organizers (word web, story maps, KWL charts), photographs, concrete materials, and graphs, for example.

# Involving English Language Learners in Music Activities

Music is a universal language that draws people together. For English language learners, music can be a powerful vehicle for language learning and community-building. Music and singing are important to second language learners for many reasons, including:

○ The rhythms of music help children hear the sounds and intonation patterns of a new language.

○ Musical lyrics and accompanying motions help children learn new vocabulary.

○ Repetitive patterns of language in songs help children internalize the sentence structure of English.

○ Important cultural information is conveyed to young children in the themes of songs.

Strategies for involving English language learners in music activities vary according to the children's level of proficiency in the English language.

| Level of Proficiency | Strategies |
| --- | --- |
| Beginning English Language Learners | o Keep the child near you and model motions as you engage in group singing.<br>o Use hand gestures, movements, and signs as often as possible to accompany song lyrics, making sure to tie a specific motion to a specific word.<br>o Refer to real objects in the environment that are named in a song.<br>o Stress the intonation, sounds, and patterns in language by speaking the lyrics of the song while performing actions or referring to objects in the environment.<br>o Use simple, more common vocabulary. For example, use *round* instead of *circular*. |
| Intermediate-Level English Language Learners | o Say the song before singing it, so children can hear the words and rhythms of the lyrics.<br>o Use motions, gestures, and signs to help children internalize the meaning of song lyrics. Be sure the motion is tied clearly to the associated word.<br>o Throughout the day, repeat the language patterns found in songs in various activities.<br>o Stress the language patterns in songs, and pause as children fill in the blanks.<br>o Adapt the patterns of song, using familiar vocabulary. |
| Advanced English Language Learners | o Use visuals to cue parts of a song.<br>o Use graphic organizers to introduce unfamiliar information.<br>o Use synonyms for words heard in songs to expand children's vocabulary.<br>o Develop vocabulary through description and comparison. For example, it is *round* like a circle. It is *circular*.<br>o Encourage children to make up new lyrics for songs. |

# How to Use This Book

Use the 25 songs on the *Fabulous Food CD* included with this book and the related activities in this book to enhance themes in your curriculum, or use them independently. Either way you have a rich treasure chest of creative ideas for your classroom.

The eight-package collection provides more than 200 songs, a perfect combination of the traditional best-loved children's songs and brand-new selections created for each theme. Keep a song in your heart and put joy in your teaching!

# Bibliography

Bulloch, K. 2003. *The mystery of modifying: Creative solutions.* Huntsville, TX: Education Service Center, Region VI.

Cavallaro, C. & M. Haney. 1999. *Preschool inclusion.* Baltimore, MD: Paul H. Brookes Publishing Company.

Gray, T. and S. Fleischman. Dec. 2004-Jan. 2005. "Research matters: Successful strategies for English language learners." *Educational Leadership,* 62, 84-85.

Hanniford, C. 1995. *Smart moves: Why learning is not all in your head.* Arlington, VA: Great Ocean Publications, p. 146.

LeDoux, J. 1993. "Emotional memory systems in the brain." *Behavioral and Brain Research,* 58.

Tabors, P. 1997. *One child, two languages: Children learning English as a second language.* Baltimore, MD: Paul H. Brookes Publishing Company.

# Songs and Activities

### Segmentation

○ Have the children clap the syllables in *peanut butter*. Have them clap the syllables in *jelly*. *Which has more syllables?*

# Curriculum Connections

### Cooking

○ Help the children make peanut butter. Place 1 cup roasted peanuts, ½ tablespoon vegetable oil, and ½ teaspoon salt in an electric blender. Blend to desired smoothness. Provide crackers and encourage the children to taste the peanut butter by spreading it on a cracker. **Safety warning:** Closely supervise the use of the blender.

 **English Language Learner Strategy:** Use a rebus (page 105) for this recipe to make it easier to follow the directions.

### Cooking/Language

○ Provide the Rebus Recipe for Peanut Butter Balls (page 106) and invite the children to follow the directions to make candy.

### Dramatic Play

○ Encourage the children to pretend that they are working in a restaurant that serves peanut butter and jelly sandwiches. Provide paper plates and squares of white (bread), tan (peanut butter), and purple (jelly) felt.

### Fine Motor

○ Invite the children to shell peanuts. Discuss different ways they might crack the shells, such as pinching the peanuts between their fingers or rolling the peanuts on the table top.

○ Make Peanut Butter Playdough. Mix together equal amounts of peanut butter and cornstarch. Encourage the children to knead the dough. Make sure children wash their hands before kneading the dough. When they have finished playing with the dough they can eat it.

### Games

○ Play Drop the Peanut as you would play Drop the Handkerchief. Have the children form a circle. Select one child to be IT. IT walks around the circle and eventually drops the peanut behind another child. The selected child chases IT around the circle and attempts to tag him before he can get back around to the child's place in the circle.

### Gross Motor

○ Mark a throw line on the floor using masking tape. Invite the children to toss peanuts into buckets.

## Language

○ Draw faces on peanut shells that have been broken in half. Encourage the children to put the shells on their fingertips and use them as puppets.

○ Give the children Peanut Butter and Jelly Sandwich Sequence Cards (page 110). Encourage them to place the cards in the correct order.

✓ **Special Needs Adaptation:** Hold up each card as you make the peanut butter sandwich with the children. The cards provide a good opportunity to reinforce the concepts *first, next,* and *last.* The first time the child uses the cards, model for him what happens by placing the first card on the table. Use the vocabulary in a short sentence. Then ask him which card he thinks will be next. Ask him to tell you what happens on that card. After he has placed each card on the table, go over each step with him using the terms, *first, next,* and *last.* Children with cognitive challenges learn better with real examples. Make a real peanut butter sandwich using the same sequence as in the cards. Remember, children with visual challenges see black-and-white line drawings more easily than detailed drawings.

## Math

○ Ask the children to shell five peanuts. Encourage them to count the number of kernels inside each shell. *Do any of the shells have more than two kernels?*

## Science

○ Discuss the peanut plant, its structure (leaf, flower, peg, fruit, and roots), and its life cycle. Plant peanuts outside when the ground is warm and there is no chance of freezing. If the weather is not agreeable, children can plant peanuts indoors in cups and transplant the plants later. Start by soaking the raw, unshelled nuts for a few days to watch them sprout. Plant two or three nuts or sprouts five to six inches deep and about one foot apart. Peanut plants can take two months from planting to harvest, but are easy to grow.

# Home Connection

○ Encourage families to discuss their favorite peanut butter recipes.

## Book Corner

*Jamberry* by Bruce Degen
*Peanut Butter and Jelly: A Play Rhyme* by Nadine Bernard Westcott
*Peanut Butter and Jelly Game* by Adam Eisenson

SONGS AND ACTIVITIES

# Have You Been to Candyland? by Pam Schiller

(Tune: Do You Know the Muffin Man?)
Have you been to Candyland,
Candyland, Candyland?
Have you been to Candyland?
We'll swing on licorice ropes. Whee! *(pretend to swing on licorice ropes)*

Have you been to Candyland,
Candyland, Candyland?
Have you been to Candyland?
We'll swim in lemonade. *(pretend to swim in lemonade)*

Have you been to Candyland,
Candyland, Candyland?
Have you been to Candyland?
We'll slide on chocolate pies. *(pretend to slide on chocolate pies)*

Candyland, Candyland,
Candyland, Candyland,
If you haven't been to Candyland,
You'll need to visit soon!

**Special Needs Adaptation:** This song provides a chance to practice gross motor skills and following directions. Explain that the song is about a pretend journey and that the motions described in the song are part of the pretend journey. Children with certain types of special needs, particularly those with autism spectrum disorder, have difficulty with abstract concepts. Before introducing the song to the whole group, go over each step with the child, explaining that if she does not understand what to do she can do something different. Remember, your objective is not how "correctly" she does the motions but that she participates and enjoys the activities. If there are too many body motions, you can adapt the song to use fewer. If a child has severe motor issues or is in a wheelchair, she can participate by doing hand motions to the song.

## Vocabulary

Candyland
chocolate pie
lemonade
licorice rope
slide
soon
swim
swing
visit

## Theme Connections

Make-Believe
Nutrition

# Did You Know?

○ Candyland™ is a popular children's game. It was introduced in 1949 by the Milton Bradley Company.

○ Candy is made by dissolving sugar in water. Different heating levels determine the type of candy: Hot temperatures make hard candy; medium heat makes soft candy; and cool temperatures make chewy candy.

○ Some 65% of American candy brands have been around for more than 50 years.

○ Halloween is the holiday with the highest candy sales, followed by Easter, Christmas, and Valentine's Day.

○ By the mid-1800s, more than 380 American factories were producing candy, mostly "penny candy," which was displayed in glass cases in general stores and sold by the piece. **Allergy Warning:** Check for allergies or food sensitivities before allowing children to participate in any activities that involve eating candy. Also, ask parents if they allow their children to eat candy.

# Literacy Links

### Oral Language

○ Discuss the movements described in the song. *How could one swing on licorice laces? Why would a chocolate pie be a good place to slide? How would it feel to swim in lemonade?*

○ Discuss words that are used to describe candy; for example, *hard*, *soft*, *chewy*, *crunchy*, *sweet*, and *chocolate*. Ask the children to think of hard candies and soft candies. Make a list of the two different types of candy on chart paper. Are the children able to think of more hard candies or more soft candies?

### Segmentation

○ Have the children clap the syllables in *candyland*. *How many syllables do you hear?* Print *candyland* on chart paper. Draw a line between *candy* and *land*. Point out that candyland is a *compound word*. Give examples of other compound words; for example, *peanut*, *birdhouse*, or *seashell*.

# Curriculum Connections

### Art
○ Cut the center out of paper plates to make lifesaver-shaped candy. Provide a variety of paint colors and encourage the children to paint their favorite color (flavor) of lifesaver.

### Cooking
○ Make No-Cook Divinity. Combine one 6-ounce package fluffy white frosting mix, ⅓ cup light corn syrup, 1 teaspoon vanilla extract, and ½ cup boiling water. Beat on high until stiff peaks form. Gradually add 1 pound confectioners' sugar, beating constantly. Spoon onto wax paper and allow to set overnight.

### Discovery
○ Provide a variety of candies. Encourage the children to sort the candy into two categories, such as candies that roll and candies that do not roll.

### Dramatic Play
○ Provide props for a candy shop; for example, pretend candy made from posterboard, cash register, bags, bins to hold candies, and so on. Invite the children to set up a pretend candy store.

### Fine Motor
○ Make pale pink, green, and yellow playdough. Use peppermint extract to scent the dough. Encourage the children to shape the dough into small round mints (balls or flat circles or both). Discuss the smell of the dough and the shape of the candy the children are making.

### Games
○ Provide a Candyland™ board game. Show the children how to play and encourage them to play the game.

### Gross Motor
○ Use masking tape to make a 10' long line on the floor. Provide children with a plastic spoon and a wrapped hard candy. Challenge them to walk the line while carrying the candy in the spoon.
○ Make "peppermint candies" by cutting circles from white poster board and using red paint to create the familiar red and white swirl pattern. Place the peppermint candies on the floor a few feet apart to create a candy path. Invite the children to hop from peppermint to peppermint.

## Book Corner

*Candyland: A Surprise Adventure* by Gail Herman

*The M & M Counting Book* by Barbara Barbieri McGrath

*Skittle Riddles Math* by Barbara Barbieri McGrath

### Language

○ Provide plastic glasses, lemons, water, sugar, ice, and the Rebus Lemonade Recipe (page 104). Invite the children to follow the rebus directions to make a glass of lemonade.

### Math

○ Provide three or four types of hard candies that are each individually wrapped. Encourage the children to use the candy to make patterns.

### Music

○ Discuss popular songs or pieces of music about candy; for example, "Candy Man," "Big Rock Candy Mountain," or "The Dance of the Sugar Plum Fairy" (from the Nutcracker). *What is a Candy Man? What is Big Rock Candy Mountain? What is a Sugar Plum Fairy?* Invite the children to dance creatively to one of the pieces of music or songs.

### Writing

○ Print *candyland* on chart paper. Provide magnetic letters and encourage the children to copy the word.

# Home Connection

○ Encourage children to interview their families about their favorite kinds of candy.
○ Encourage the children to talk about their family's favorite candy at school.

# Chew, Chew, Chew Your Food by Pam Schiller

(Tune: Row, Row, Row Your Boat)
Chew, chew, chew your food,
A little at a time.
Chew it slow, chew it well,
Chew it to this rhyme.

Drink, drink, drink your milk
A little at a time.
Drink it slow, drink it fast.
Drink it to this rhyme.

## Vocabulary

chew

drink

fast

little

rhyme

slow

well

## Theme Connections

Health and Safety

Nutrition

## Did You Know?

○ Milk contains many nutrients that are important for health; for example, protein, vitamin A, vitamin D, riboflavin, and calcium. Calcium and vitamin D are important for building strong bones and teeth. During childhood and the teen years, the body stores calcium in bones. Adults, on the other hand, lose calcium from their bones. Adult bones stay stronger if a lot of calcium is stored during earlier years.

○ The sugar in milk—lactose—is hard to digest for some people, who may get gas and other stomach troubles when they drink milk. This is called lactose intolerance.

○ Preschool children should drink two cups of milk every day. Children who are hesitant to drink milk may enjoy flavored milk, such as strawberry or chocolate.

○ Digestion is the physical and chemical process that breaks down food into smaller and simpler compounds so the body can use them. In larger, more complex animals digestion begins in the mouth. Chewing food breaks food into smaller parts. The increased surface area of the food enables the enzymes that break down food into simpler substances to work more quickly.

○ Eating slowly and chewing food longer allows the enzymes in saliva to begin to digest the food before it enters the stomach. Food should be chewed to the consistency of mush.

# Literacy Links

## Oral Language

○ Talk about the importance of drinking milk and chewing food slowly. Discuss the added importance of chewing food well and the importance of teeth.

○ Discuss the nutritional value of milk. (**Note:** If there are children who are allergic to milk, talk about good alternatives for them.)

○ Talk about table manners, including chewing with your mouth closed, drinking slowly, not stuffing food into your mouth, and saying "please" and "thank you."

○ Teach the children the American Sign Language signs for *chew* and *drink* (page 116). Encourage them to use the signs when singing the song.

## Phonological Awareness

○ Discuss the rhyming words *time* and *rhyme*. Encourage the children to think of other words that rhyme with *time* and *rhyme*.

## Print Awareness

○ Print either verse of the song on chart paper. Move your hand under the words as the children sing the song. Point out the top-to-bottom and left-to-right movements.

**Allergy Warning:** Check for allergies before allowing children to participate in any activities that require the intake of milk or milk products.

# Curriculum Connections

## Art

○ Provide chalk, paper, and buttermilk. Place a tablespoon of buttermilk on each paper. Have the children dip a piece of chalk into the buttermilk before drawing. The buttermilk will cause the chalk to act more like paint than chalk.

## Cooking

○ Invite the children to make Purple Cow Shakes. Provide one small scoop of vanilla ice cream and 2 tablespoons of grape juice concentrate in a small plastic baby food jar. Have the children shake their jars, pour their shakes into cups, and enjoy.

**English Language Learner Strategy:** Use a rebus (page 107) for this recipe to make it easier for English language learners to follow the directions.

### Discovery

❍ Provide tools for grinding food, such as choppers, mashers, grinders, and graters. Provide playdough. Encourage the children to explore the tools to determine which one works best to get the playdough broken into smaller parts. **Safety Warning:** This activity requires adult supervision.

❍ Provide three small peeled potatoes, three plastic glasses, a grater, a plastic knife, and peroxide. **Caution:** Only adults should handle the peroxide. Have the children place one whole potato in the first glass and label it #1. Help them slice the second potato, place it in the second glass, and label it #2. Help them grate the third potato, place the grated pieces in the last glass, and label it #3. Place 2 tablespoons of peroxide in each glass (adult only). Watch the reaction. Explain that this is similar to what happens to food in our stomach. The last glass shows what

 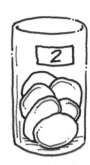 

happen to food that is well-chewed. The more we chew food, the smaller it gets and the more easily the enzymes in our mouth and in our stomach can break it down. Eating slowly and chewing food longer allows the enzymes in saliva to begin to digest the food before it enters the stomach. **Safety Warning:** This activity requires adult participation and supervision.

### Dramatic Play

❍ Provide baby dolls, bottles, empty baby food jars, spoons, and other props so the children can pretend to feed babies. Encourage them to sing the song as they feed the babies.

### Science

❍ Remind the children that their teeth are essential tools to help our stomachs digest food. Provide photos of teeth. Help the children make Homemade Toothpaste by mixing 1 teaspoon baking soda, 3 or 4 drops peppermint extract, and enough water to create a paste. Provide toothbrushes and encourage the children to brush their teeth.

### Snack/Math

❍ Provide flavored milk for snack. Encourage the children to select their favorite flavor: plain, chocolate, or strawberry. Graph their choices. Provide cookies to accompany the milk. Ask the children to count the number of times they chew each bite of their cookie. Graph the results.

**Book Corner**

*Guts: Our Digestive System* by Seymour Simon

*Why Not Call It Cow Juice?* by Steven Krasner

Which milk is their favorite? What was the most frequently reported number of chews?

## Water Play

○ Provide a variety of tools for pouring water; for example, pitchers, eyedroppers, basters, and funnels. *Which tools move water quickly? Which tools move the water slowly?*

✓ **Special Needs Adaptation:** Encourage the children to work with peer buddies or in a small collaborative group. Every child in the class might enjoy completing this activity with a buddy. For children with special needs, you might assign a specific peer buddy, especially if you know a child who will be patient and encourage his friend to participate. You may also ask children to volunteer to be a peer buddy. When asking for a peer-buddy volunteer, use the child's name; for example, say, "Who would like to be a buddy with Micah for this activity?" Sometimes children with special needs will select their own peer buddies.

## Writing

○ Trace magnetic letters to write *chew* and *drink* on large index cards. Invite the children to place magnetic letters over the words on the index cards.

# Home Activities

○ Encourage the children to tell their families why it is so important to chew your food well.
○ Encourage the children to bring pictures of their favorite foods from home.

# The Donut Song

Oh, I ran around the corner,
And I ran around the block,
I ran right into the bakery shop.
I grabbed me a donut right out of the grease,
And I handed the lady a five-cent piece.
She looked at the nickel, and she looked at me.
She said, "This nickel is no good to me.
There's a hole in the nickel and it goes right through."
Said I, "There's a hole in your donut, too!
Thanks for the donut.
Good-bye!"

## Vocabulary

bakery shop
block
corner
donut
five-cent piece
grabbed
grease
hole
nickel

## Theme Connections

Community Workers
Nutrition

## Did You Know?

○ The hole in the donut has been attributed to the Pennsylvania Dutch and to a New England sea captain. Neither were the first. Archaeologists have found petrified fried cakes with holes in the center in prehistoric Native American ruins in the Southwestern United States. Donuts have been "invented" more than once!

○ Which has more calories and fat, and why—a plain sugared donut with a hole in the middle, or a round jelly-filled donut? Jelly donuts have fewer calories and less fat than plain donuts with holes. While a plain donut with a hole might weigh less, it has more surface area exposed to the cooking oil than a round donut.

## Literacy Links

### Letter Knowledge
○ Print *hole* and *whole* on chart paper. Read the words for the children. Tell them that although the words sound the same, they have different meanings. Define each word. Ask the children which letter is different in each word.

### Oral Language
○ Ask children why they think that donuts have a hole in the center. List their ideas on chart paper.

○ Tell the children that donuts exist in many countries. In Mexico they are called *pan du dulce*. In France they are called *beignets*. Discuss the many names for donuts.

### Phonological Awareness

○ Print the following tongue twister on chart paper: *Donut dunkers dunk donuts*. Point out that each word in this sentence starts with the letter "d." Explain that when several words with the same beginning letter are grouped together in a phrase or a sentence, the repetitive sound is called *alliteration*. Have the children say the tongue twister three times quickly. What happens?

# Curriculum Connections

### Art

○ Cut poster board into circles with holes in the middle to make donut shapes. Provide paint, crayons, and colored glue. Encourage the children to paint or color their donuts. Show them how to use squeeze bottles of colored glue to decorate the donuts.

### Cooking

○ Invite the children to make donuts. Give each child a refrigerator biscuit. Provide a soda bottle cap to use as a "hole cutter." Place the donuts in a small fryer. **Caution**: Only adults put the donuts in the fryer, turn them, and take them out of the fryer. Fry for three minutes on each side or until golden brown. Provide powdered sugar and encourage the children to sprinkle their donuts while they are cooling. **Safety Warning:** This activity requires adult participation and supervision.

### Dramatic Play

○ Provide props for a bakery shop; for example, playdough, rolling pins, pans, trays, aprons, cash register, play money, and other props. Encourage the children to pretend they are preparing donuts for a bakery.

✓ **English Language Learner Strategy:** Dramatic play provides many opportunities for developing language skills. At the same time, it is possible for children to participate nonverbally in dramatic play situations. Interact with children while they play. Provide vocabulary assistance as appropriate.

## Book Corner

*Arnie, the Doughnut* by Laurie Keller
*Around the World With the Donut Man* by Lise Caldwell

### Field Trip

○ Visit a donut shop. *How many different donuts do they make? Do all the donuts have holes?*

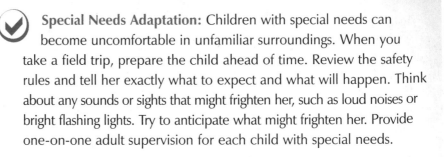 **Special Needs Adaptation:** Children with special needs can become uncomfortable in unfamiliar surroundings. When you take a field trip, prepare the child ahead of time. Review the safety rules and tell her exactly what to expect and what will happen. Think about any sounds or sights that might frighten her, such as loud noises or bright flashing lights. Try to anticipate what might frighten her. Provide one-on-one adult supervision for each child with special needs.

### Fine Motor

○ Provide playdough and decorative items, such as, buttons, beads, and sequins. Encourage the children to make and decorate donuts.

### Games

○ Play Toss the Donut. Cut the center from five plastic coffee can lids to make pretend "donuts." Pour sand into an empty 2-liter soda bottle and use it for a stake. Create a throw line with masking tape. Challenge the children to toss the "donuts" and attempt to ring the stake.

### Math

○ Provide Cheerios or a similar-shaped cereal that children can use to represent donuts. Write one numeral from 1-5 on each of five plates or, if available, small pans. Have the children count the correct number of "donuts" (cereal) into the pans.

**Special Needs Adaptation:** Adapt this activity to match the skills of an individual child. For example, if a child has only learned number concepts up to three, provide three plates.

### Outdoors

○ Provide an old tire or an inner tube to represent a donut and a ball to represent a donut hole. Challenge the children to toss the ball ("donut hole") through the "donut." If possible, hang the tire from a tree.

# Home Connection

○ Encourage families to visit a donut shop.

# Bread and Jelly by Pam Schiller

## Vocabulary

| | |
|---|---|
| bread | cake |
| chocolate | fries |
| ice cream | gravy |
| ketchup | jelly |
| like | milk |
| potato | |

## Theme Connections

Nutrition

Things That Go
   Together

(Tune: London Bridge Is Falling Down)

I like jelly on my bread,
On my bread, on my bread.
I like jelly on my bread.
Bread and jelly!

I like ice cream with my cake,
With my cake, with my cake.
I like ice cream with my cake.
Cake and ice cream!

I like gravy on my potatoes,
On my potatoes, on my potatoes.
I like gravy on my potatoes.
Potatoes and gravy!

I like ketchup on my fries,
On my fries, on my fries.
I like ketchup on my fries.
Fries and ketchup!

I like chocolate in my milk,
In my milk, in my milk.
I like chocolate in my milk.
Chocolate milk!

# Did You Know?

- Breaking bread is a universal sign of peace.
- Each American consumes an average of 53 pounds of bread per year.
- It takes nine seconds for a combine to harvest enough wheat to make 70 loaves of bread. One bushel of wheat will produce 73 one-pound loaves of bread.
- Americans consume the most ice cream in the world per capita, with Australians coming in second. In 1924, the average American ate eight pints of ice cream a year. By 1997, the International Dairy Foods Association reported that the figure had jumped to 48 pints a year.
- The most avid ice cream eaters live in Omaha, Nebraska. They ate more ice cream per person than other Americans.
- Vanilla is the most popular ice cream flavor in this country, accounting for 20 to 29 percent of all ice cream sales. Chocolate comes in a distant second, with about 10 percent of the market.
- American chocolate manufacturers use 1.5 billion pounds of milk, surpassed only by the cheese and ice cream industries. **Allergy Warning:** Check for allergies and food sensitivities before serving any food.

# Literacy Links

### Oral Language
○  Discuss things that go together. Make a list of pairs of things that children mention.

> ✓ **English Language Learner Strategy:** For children who are beginning English language learners, provide pictures of things that go together and ask the child to sort the pictures into piles of things that go together.

### Print Awareness/Oral Language
○  Make a list of things that people put on fries, such as ketchup, mustard, cheese, salt, chili, and vinegar.

# Curriculum Connections

### Art
○  Encourage the children to draw pictures of things that go together.

### Discovery
○  Provide photos of animals and their homes. Encourage the children to match each animal to its home.
○  Provide photos of animals and their babies. Encourage the children to match the mother to her baby.

### Games
○  Give the children a box of classroom items (a CD, pencil, puzzle piece, and so on) without the items that go with them (a CD player, pencil sharpener or holder, and a puzzle). Have them look around the classroom for items to go with the items in the box.

### Language
○  Give the children the Things That Go Together Matching Cards (page 112). Encourage them to match items that go together.
○  Provide a basket of items that go together (bucket and shovel, brush and comb, shoe and laces, dog and bone, toothpaste and toothbrush, and so on). Encourage the children to match the items that go together.

## Oral Language

○ Discuss muffins. Ask the children to name different types of muffins, and make a list of the muffins.

## Phonological Awareness

○ Print *muffin man* on chart paper. Point out that when the first letter of two or more words in a row is the same, the sound they make is called *alliteration*. Print the following tongue twister on chart paper: *The muffin man makes magic muffins*. Underline the letter "m" at the beginning of each word. Challenge the children to say the tongue twister three times quickly.

**Special Needs Adaptation:** Children with cognitive challenges may not learn letter sounds as quickly as other children. The letter "m" is easy to teach because it is the first letter in the word "me" which most children know. Demonstrate how the /m/ sound is made by placing your lips together. Encourage the child to make the /m/ sound with you. Tell him that the /m/ sound is the sound we make when something we like to eat smells good. Provide cutouts of the letter "m" for the child to touch and feel while you are doing the chart paper activities described above. While the child may not understand the concept of alliteration, he can tell you words he knows that start with the letter "m". Throughout the day, look for opportunities to talk about and point out things you see that start with the letter "m".

# Curriculum Connections

## Blocks

○ Have the children build buildings along a road that you mark as Drury Lane. Encourage them to build a bakery on Drury Lane.

## Dramatic Play

○ Provide props for a muffin bakery and shop; for example, aprons, rolling pins, playdough, empty muffin mix boxes and packages, and muffin tins. Encourage the children to set up a bakery and shop that specializes in muffins. Help them create signs for their shop, including a Drury Lane street sign.

## Book Corner

*If You Give a Moose a Muffin* by Laura Joffe Numeroff

*Jamberry* by Bruce Degen

*Muffin Dragon* by Stephen Cosgrove

✓ **English Language Learner Strategy:** Dramatic play provides many opportunities for developing language skills. At the same time, it is possible to participate nonverbally in dramatic play.

### Field Trip

❍ Take a trip to a local bakery. Make a list of the muffins available at the bakery. Talk with the baker about which muffins are the favorite of most customers.

### Fine Motor

❍ Provide paper cupcake holders, tweezers, and small beads to represent blueberries. Invite the children to use the tweezers to pick up the beads and place them into the cupcake holders.

### Games

❍ Play Muffin Man Says as you would play Simon Says. Give directions to the children. Tell them they should only respond to directions preceded by the words, "Muffin Man says..."

### Language

❍ Print *muffin* on chart paper. Print several copies of the letters *m*, *u*, *f*, *i*, and *n* on the bottoms of paper cupcake holders. Encourage the children to spell *muffin* using the paper cupcake holders.

### Math

❍ Use the muffin pattern (page 115) to create 15 muffins. Write one numeral from 1-5 on each of five paper plates. Encourage the children to place the number of muffins on each plate that corresponds with the numeral on the plate.

### Snack

❍ Provide a variety of muffins for children to taste. Be sure to include English muffins. Discuss the muffins. Ask questions. *Which muffin do you like best? Which muffins have a grainy texture? Which muffin has a texture that is smooth?* Discuss what texture means. *Are muffins a healthier food than donuts? Why? How are muffins and cupcakes alike? How are they different?*

# Home Connection

❍ Suggest that children interview their family members, asking them to name their favorite muffins.

# Oats, Peas, Beans, and Barley Grow

## Vocabulary

anyone
barley
beans
grow
oats
peas

## Theme Connections

Farms
Growing Things
Nutrition

Oats, peas, beans, and barley grow.
Oats, peas, beans, and barley grow.
Not you or I or anyone knows,
How oats, peas, beans, and barley grow?

## Did You Know?

○ Oats are a cereal grain used primarily as food for livestock. Only 5% of the world crop is consumed by humans. The plants make excellent straw, and the hulls are a source of the chemical *furfural*, an industrial solvent.

○ Quaker Oats in Cedar Rapids, Iowa is the largest cereal company in the world.

○ Peas are a cool season, annual crop planted in rotation with other crops, such as potatoes, sweet corn, and snap beans. Peas are members of the legume family and provide a good source of protein.

○ Beans have been part of the human diet since prehistoric times. They are a source of folic acid and vitamin C.

○ The young barley leaf is a green cereal grass that contains the highest and most balanced concentration of nutrients found in nature. Barley is a major food and animal feed crop. It is the fifth largest cultivated cereal crop in the world.

○ Barley was one of the earliest cereal foods used by humankind. Barley cereal is one of the first solid foods recommended for babies.

## Literacy Links

### Oral Language

○ Discuss oats, peas, beans, and barley and how each is used.

 **English Language Learner Strategy:** Show the children the empty packaging for oats, peas, beans, and barley.

○  Teach the children "Peas Porridge Hot." Discuss the many different ways we eat peas.

**Peas Porridge Hot**

*Peas porridge hot!*       *Some like it hot.*
*Peas porridge cold!*       *Some like it cold.*
*Peas porridge in the pot*     *Some like in the pot*
*Nine days old.*         *Nine days old!*

## Print Awareness

○  Print the song on chart paper. Point to the words as the children sing the song. Point out the left-to-right and top-to-bottom movement of the words.

> ✔ **Special Needs Adaptation:** Pointing out the left-to-right and top-to-bottom movement of the words is an important pre-literacy concept for children with special needs. It is important that they understand that words follow a set of patterns. It is also important to demonstrate that books follow patterns; for example, a book is read from front to back and the pages of a book are turned from right to left. Draw arrows above each word as a cue that words go from left to right.

## Segmentation

○  Clap *oats, peas, beans,* and *barley. Which word has the most syllables?*

> ✔ **Special Needs Adaptation:** Clapping out the syllables helps children with special needs work on fine motor and math skills. If the child has difficulty understanding how to clap each syllable, clap each word for him and then ask him to clap along with you. For some children you may need to clap one syllable, stop, and then ask him to clap. Children with motor challenges can use alternatives to clapping, such as tapping on a lid or a drum.

# Curriculum Connections

## Art

○  Provide green paint and easel paper. Encourage the children to paint green plants.

## Discovery

○  Provide oats, peas, beans, and barley so the children can examine each type of grain and legume. Provide a magnifying glass so children can see the grains and legumes close up.

### Field Trip

○ Take a trip to a local farm. *Can you find each of the items mentioned in the song?*

### Fine Motor

○ Provide a pastry brush, beans, a bucket or a cup, and a scoop. Have the children sweep the beans into the scoop and dump them into the bucket or cup. When the children are finished, wash the beans and cook them.

### Gross Motor

○ Invite the children to create a hand jive (clapping pattern) for the rhyme, "Peas Porridge Hot" (in Literacy Links).

### Science

○ Invite each child to plant a bean. Each child places a lima bean inside a wet paper towel and then inside a plastic resealable bag. When the beans begin to sprout, remove them and plant each in a cup of potting soil. As the bean sprouts grow, invite the children to care for them. Encourage the children to measure the height of their plants from time to time.

### Snack

○ Prepare instant oatmeal for the children and invite them to flavor their oatmeal with brown sugar, strawberries, peaches, or other seasoning or fruit.

### Writing

○ Print *oats, peas, beans,* and *barley* on separate index cards. Provide magnetic letters and encourage the children to use the letters to copy the names of the grains and legumes on the index cards.

✓ **English Language Learner Strategy:** Provide real objects, such as oats, peas, beans, and barley, for reference. Provide pictures of oats, peas, beans, and barley growing in a field or garden.

*Eating the Alphabet: Fruits and Vegetables From A to Z* by Lois Ehlert
*Growing Vegetable Soup* by Lois Ehlert

# Home Connection

○ Encourage the families to find products in their homes that are made with oats, peas, beans, and barley. Are they able to find each of the items mentioned in the song?

# Goober Peas

Sitting by the roadside on a summer's day
Chatting with my buddies, passing time away
Lying in the shadows underneath the trees
Goodness, how delicious, eating goober peas.

Peas, peas, peas, peas
Eating goober peas,
Goodness, how delicious,
Eating goober peas.

**Allergy Warning:** Check allergies before allowing children to eat peanuts or participate in any activities involving peanuts.

✓ **English Language Learner Strategy:** Use hand gestures, movements, or signs to accompany the song lyrics, making sure to tie a specific motion to a specific word.

## Vocabulary

buddies
chatting
delicious
goober peas
passing
roadside
shadow
summer
tree

## Theme Connections

Growing Things
Nutrition

## Did You Know?

○ The term *goober peas* is one of many names for peanuts. Before the Civil War, peanuts were known throughout the South as *groundnuts, ground peas, goober peas, monkey nuts, pindars,* and *goobers.*
○ The peanut is not a nut; it is a legume, which is related to beans and lentils.
○ Peanuts account for two-thirds of all snack nuts consumed in the United States, and four of the top 10 candy bars manufactured in the United States contain peanuts or peanut butter.
○ The average American consumes more than six pounds of peanuts and peanut butter products each year.
○ March is National Peanut Month.

## Literacy Links

### Letter Knowledge

○ Print *goober peas* on chart paper. Ask the children to name the letters in the two words. *Which letters appear more than once?*

## Oral Language

○ Make a Word Web. Print *goober peas* in the center of a sheet of chart paper. Draw a circle around the words. Ask the children to tell you everything they know about peanuts. Write their information on lines that extend outward from the circle.

○ Sing "Found a Peanut" with the children.

### Found a Peanut

*Found a peanut, found a peanut,*      *Cracked it open, cracked it open,*
*Found a peanut just now,*      *Cracked it open just now,*
*Just now I found a peanut,*      *Just now I cracked it open,*
*Found a peanut just now.*      *Cracked it open just now.*

*Additional verses:*
*It was rotten, it was rotten…*
*Ate it anyway, ate it anyway…*
*Got a stomach ache, got a stomach ache…*
*Called the doctor, called the doctor…*
*Died anyway, died anyway…*
*Went to heaven, went to heaven…*
*Was a dream, was a dream…*
*Then I woke up, then I woke up...*
*Found a peanut, found a peanut…*

# Curriculum Connections

## Art

○ Provide fingerpaint and paper. Show the children how to use two thumbprints to make peanuts.

## Discovery

○ Pour fingerpaint directly on a tabletop. Place empty peanut shell halves on the ends of children's fingers on their right hand. Invite them to fingerpaint directly on the tabletop. *How does the paint feel on each hand? What special marks can you make with the shells?*

## Fine Motor

○ Provide "goober peas" for children to shell.

## Book Corner

*From Peanut to Peanut Butter* by Robin Nelson
*Make Me a Peanut Butter Sandwich and a Glass of Milk* by Ken Robbins
*Peanut Butter and Jelly: A Play Rhyme* by Nadine Bernard Westcott

### Games

○ Invite children to play Hide the Peanut. Hide a peanut and invite the children to find it.

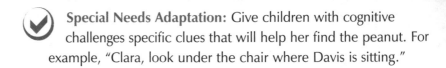

**Special Needs Adaptation:** Give children with cognitive challenges specific clues that will help her find the peanut. For example, "Clara, look under the chair where Davis is sitting."

### Gross Motor

○ Provide peanuts in the shell and a bucket. Create a throw line by placing a strip of masking tape on the floor. Challenge the children to toss the peanuts into the bucket. When the game is over, invite the children to eat the peanuts.

### Language

○ Provide the Rebus Directions for Trail Mix (page 108). Provide pretzels, miniature marshmallows, cereal, and peanuts. Invite the children to follow the recipe to make trail mix for their snack.

### Math

○ Copy the Peanut Pattern (page 113). Write one numeral from 1-5 on each of five plastic baby food jars. Cut a slit in each lid. **Caution**: This is an adult-only step. Invite the children to place the same number of peanut patterns into the jars as the numeral printed on the jar. Encourage the children to count the peanut patterns as they place them in the jars.

### Writing

○ Print *goober peas* on index cards. Print the letters *g, o, b, e, r, p, a,* and *s* on the Peanut Pattern (page 113). Encourage the children to arrange the peanuts to spell *goober peas.*

**Special Needs Adaptation:** Adapt this activity by asking the child to arrange the letters to form the word peas rather than goober peas. Say each letter and ask him to repeat each letter after you.

# Home Connection

○ Have the children ask their families what name they use for peanuts.

# The Watermelon Song

## Vocabulary

head
juice
rind
slip
slurp
Southern fried chicken
through
watermelon

## Theme Connections

Growing Things
Nutrition

Just put a watermelon
Right over your head,
And let the juice
(Slurp) slip through.
Just put a watermelon
Right over your head,
That's all I ask of you.
Now Southern fried chicken

Might taste mighty fine,
But nothin' tastes better
Than a watermelon rind.
So, put a watermelon
Right over your head,
And let the juice
(Slurp) slip through!

✓ **Special Needs Adaptation:** The vocabulary associated with this song will be difficult for children with language delays and cognitive challenges. Show the children a real watermelon. Show the children the parts of the fruit—the rind, the seeds, the flesh, and so on. Southern fried chicken is a specific (way to cook) chicken. Bring in pictures of fried chicken for the child to see. The meaning of slurp may also be difficult; demonstrate the meaning of the word by slurping water from a cup. It might be fun for the child to slurp water, too. Explain that you are playing around when you slurp and that slurping is not the proper way to drink liquids.

# Did You Know?

○ Watermelon is grown in more than 96 countries worldwide, and more than 1,200 varieties are grown worldwide.

○ In China and Japan, watermelon is a popular gift to bring to a host. In Israel and Egypt, the sweet taste of watermelon is often paired with the salty taste of feta cheese.

○ Watermelon is 92% water.

○ Watermelon is a vegetable! It is related to cucumbers, pumpkins, and squash.

○ By weight, watermelon is the most-consumed melon in the United States, followed by cantaloupe and honeydew. In 2001, over 4 billion pounds of watermelon were produced in the United States.

○ Early explorers used watermelons as canteens.

○ In 1990, Bill Carson of Arrington, Tennessee grew a watermelon that weighed 262 pounds!

○ Watermelon is an ideal health food because it does not contain any fat or cholesterol. It is an excellent source of vitamins A, B[6], and C, and contains fiber and potassium.

# Literacy Links

### Comprehension

❍ Invite the children to use *watermelon* in a sentence.

### Oral Language

❍ Print *watermelon* on chart paper. Draw a line between *water* and *melon*. Point out that the word watermelon is made up of two words—*water* and *melon*. Tell the children that when a word is made up of two words, it is called a *compound word*. Provide examples of other compound words, such as *milkshake*, *baseball*, and *doghouse*.

### Phonological Awareness

❍ Discuss *slurp*. Explain that it is a word that sounds like the sound it is describing. It is an *onomatopoeic* word. *What other words might we use to describe sipping watermelon juice?*

### Segmentation

❍ Have the children clap the syllables in *watermelon*. Challenge them to think of another vegetable that has three syllables, such as potato, cucumber, or broccoli.

# Curriculum Connections

### Art

❍ Cut easel paper into ovals. Provide pink, light green, and dark green paint, and invite the children to paint watermelons.

### Discovery

❍ Provide round objects, such as balls, marbles, candies, and peas along with oval-shaped objects, such as, plastic eggs, lemons, candies, and beans. Invite the children to sort the shapes.

### Fine Motor

❍ Cut hot pink (or dark pink) sponges into cubes. Provide the sponge cubes and tongs. Invite the children to move the sponges from one dish to another using the tongs.

### Gross Motor

❍ Give the children watermelon seeds and plastic cups. Have them stand about three feet away from the cup and toss their seeds into it.

○ Wad up green bulletin board paper to create watermelons. Place them on the floor, with each bulletin board watermelon as an obstacle. Have the children make their way through the maze of watermelons by jumping over them.

## Language

○ Make photocopies of the Seed-to-Fruit Sequence Cards (page 111). Color them, cut them out, and laminate them. Invite the children to sequence the cards from seed to vegetable.

○ Print *watermelon* on 4" by 12" stripes of poster board leaving a small space between *water* and *melon*. Add picture clues under each word; for example, a cup of water under *water* and a melon under *melon*. Laminate each strip, and then make puzzle cuts between the words *water* and *melon*. Invite the children to put the words back together.

## Math

○ Make watermelon slices by cutting hot pink construction paper into ovals and then cutting the ovals in half. Cut a sheet of green construction paper and use it to create a rind around one edge of the oval. Print one numeral 1-10 on each watermelon slice. Provide tweezers and watermelon seeds. Encourage the children to use the tweezers to place the correct number of seeds on each slice to match the numeral.

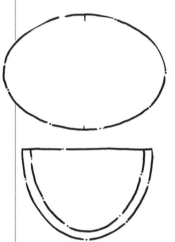

## Science

○ Plant watermelon seeds. They are easy to grow if you have rich soil and a warm climate.

## Snack

○ Serve watermelon for snack. Discuss the parts of the watermelon, such as the rind, the fruit (flesh), and the seeds.

○ Invite the children to use the Watermelon Smoothie Rebus Recipe (page 109) to make a snack.

*Anansi and the Talking Melon* by Eric A. Kimmel
*Down by the Bay* by Raffi
*Icy Watermelon* by Sandia Fria
*Watermelon Day* by Kathi Appelt

# Home Connection

○ Send Seed-to-Fruit Sequence cards (page 111) home with the children. Ask them to explain the growing sequence to their families.

# One Bottle of Pop

*(First sing entire song together, then in a round)*

One bottle of pop,
Two bottles of pop,
Three bottles of pop,
Four bottles of pop,
Five bottles of pop,
Six bottles of pop,
Seven bottles of pop, POP!
Fish and chips and vinegar,
Vinegar, vinegar.
Fish and chips and vinegar.
Pepper, pepper, pepper, salt!
Don't throw your junk
In my backyard,
My backyard, my backyard.
Don't throw your junk
In my backyard,
My backyard's full!

## Vocabulary

backyard
bottle of pop
chips
fish
junk
pepper
salt
vinegar

## Theme Connections

Counting
Growing Things
Nutrition

## Did You Know?

- The first soda pop made in the United States was Vernor's Ginger Ale, created in Detroit, Michigan in 1866. Coca Cola, Hires Root Beer, and Dr. Pepper were all introduced in 1886.
- Fish and chips are a traditional seaside meal. It is thought to be the quintessential British meal, but new research claims fish and chips are originally Jewish and French, a mixture of French *frites* and Jewish fish dishes.

## Literacy Links

### Oral Language

- Make a list of different terms that are used for soda; for example, *pop, soda water, coke, soft drink, fizzy water, cold drink,* and so on.
- Describe *fish and chips*. Discuss different ways to eat fish. *Who eats it with vinegar? Does anyone eat it with lemon juice? What about tartar sauce?*

# Hamburger

## adapted by Richele Bartkowiak and Pam Schiller

### Vocabulary

craziest       green
hamburger    ketchup
mayonnaise   mustard
pickle          rainbow
red             spread
tomato         white
yellow

### Theme Connections

Colors
Counting

Sound off!
1, 2!
Sound off!
3, 4!
Bring it on down!
1, 2, 3, 4!
1, 2!
3, 4!

Mustard, mustard sure is yellow!
Mustard, mustard sure is yellow!
Can I get that with a side of Jell-O?
Can I get that with a side of Jell-O?

Mayonnaise, mayonnaise sure is
    white!
Mayonnaise, mayonnaise sure is
    white!
Spread it on, it tastes just right!
Spread it on, it tastes just right!

Ketchup, ketchup sure is red!
Ketchup, ketchup sure is red!
I think I'll have a tomato instead!
I think I'll have a tomato instead!

Pickles, pickles sure are green!
Pickles, pickles sure are green!
Craziest things I've ever seen!
Craziest things I've ever seen!

Hamburger's my favorite meal!
Hamburger's my favorite meal!
A rainbow of colors, what a deal!
A rainbow of colors, what a deal!

## Did You Know?

o  "Hamburger" is a marching chant.
o  Americans consumed more than 13 billion hamburgers in 2003. Seven
    out of every ten hamburgers consumed in the United States were
    prepared and purchased outside the home.
o  Saturday is the biggest hamburger day in restaurants. In 2003, 1.4 billion
    hamburgers were eaten on Saturdays.
o  June is the biggest hamburger month in restaurants. In 2003, nearly 800
    million burgers were ordered and eaten in restaurants in June.
o  Hamburger is the most popular food for the grill, followed by steak and
    chicken. One out of every five times Americans fire up the grill, it is to
    cook a hamburger.
o  The first restaurant chain to serve hamburgers was White Castle in
    Wichita, Kansas in 1921.

# Literacy Links

### Oral Language

○ Teach the children the American Sign Language sign for *hamburger* (page 116).

○ Discuss hamburgers. *Where do you like to buy hamburgers? What do you like on your hamburger? Who likes cheese on their burger?*

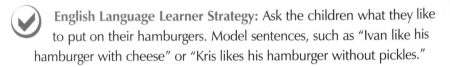 **English Language Learner Strategy:** Ask the children what they like to put on their hamburgers. Model sentences, such as "Ivan like his hamburger with cheese" or "Kris likes his hamburger without pickles."

### Phonological Awareness

○ Print some of the song's rhyming word pairs on chart paper; for example, *deal* and *meal*, *green* and *seen*, and so on. Ask the children to think of other words that rhyme with each pair.

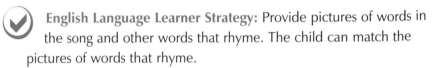 **English Language Learner Strategy:** Provide pictures of words in the song and other words that rhyme. The child can match the pictures of words that rhyme.

# Curriculum Connections

### Art

○ Provide paint to match the colors mentioned in the song. Encourage children to paint a hamburger or a rainbow.

### Discovery

○ Provide prisms. Invite the children to make rainbows with the prisms. *Can you find the colors mentioned in the song in the rainbow?*

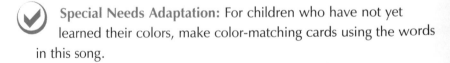 **Special Needs Adaptation:** For children who have not yet learned their colors, make color-matching cards using the words in this song.

### Dramatic Play

○ Provide props, such as an apron, a spatula, a cash register and play money, ingredients for a hamburger (if plastic items are not available, cut out items from felt), and empty mustard, mayonnaise, and ketchup containers to set up a pretend hamburger stand. Include items needed for making a hamburger. Invite the children to pretend to make and sell hamburgers.

# Hot Cross Buns

## Vocabulary

buy          light
currant      penny
fresh        sweet
hot cross bun

## Theme Connections

Community Workers
Counting
Nutrition

Hot cross buns,
One a penny buns.
One a penny,
Two a penny,
Hot cross buns.

Fresh, sweet buns,
Come and buy my buns;
One a penny,
Two a penny,
Fresh, sweet buns.

Nice, light buns,
Buy my currant buns;
Come and try them,
Then you'll buy them,
Nice, light buns.

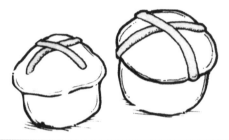

## Did You Know?

○ Hot cross buns are a spicy currant or raisin-studded yeast bun, topped with lemon flavored icing in a cross shape.

○ In England, hot cross buns are a favorite traditional treat on Good Friday. This tradition has spread to America.

○ Hot cross buns were once sold by street vendors in England who advertised their wares with cries of "Hot cross buns! Hot cross buns!" These cries are used in this nursery rhyme, "Hot Cross Buns."

○ A penny in Tudor England was a silver coin at the time in which this song was created. The abbreviation for a Tudor English penny is *d*. In 1971, the symbol for a British penny symbol became *p*.

## Literacy Links

### Oral Language

○ Discuss street vendors and variations of street vendors, such as the person who drives the ice cream truck. Ask the children if they know someone who sells food or drinks on the street (such as a hot dog or snow cone stand) or in a truck (such as an ice cream truck) that travels from home to home. *Why do people sell food in these spots? Who buys the food?*

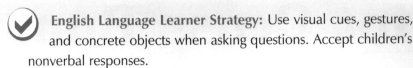 **English Language Learner Strategy:** Use visual cues, gestures, and concrete objects when asking questions. Accept children's nonverbal responses.

### Segmentation

○ Invite the children to clap the syllables of the words in the first verse of the song. *Which word has more than one syllable?*

# Curriculum Connections

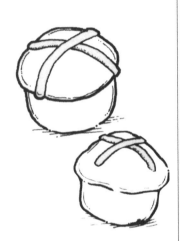

### Dramatic Play

○ Provide props for a bakery; for example, aprons, hats, rolling pins, playdough, cookie sheets, and so on. Encourage the children to set up a pretend bakery.

### Field Trip

○ Take a trip to a local bakery. *Does the bakery sell hot cross buns?*

### Fine Motor

○ Provide playdough and plastic knives. Invite the children to shape buns and then use the knives to make crosses on top of the buns.

### Fine Motor/Art

○ Provide food magazines and encourage children to cut or tear out photos of rolls and breads to create a collage.

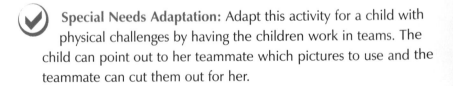 **Special Needs Adaptation:** Adapt this activity for a child with physical challenges by having the children work in teams. The child can point out to her teammate which pictures to use and the teammate can cut them out for her.

### Music and Movement

○ Challenge the children to work with a partner to create a "partner patty cake" to go with the song.

### Outdoors/Dramatic Play

○ Make pretend hot cross buns with playdough (see the Fine Motor activity) and place them on a tray. Put the tray in a wagon. Encourage the children to be vendors selling their pastries. Remind them that they must recite the rhyme to let customers know what they are selling.

## Book Corner

*Bread, Bread, Bread* by Ann Morris
*Bread Is for Eating* by David Gershator
*Everybody Bakes Bread* by Nora Dooley
*The Little Red Hen* by Paul Galdone
*Sun Bread* by Elisa Kleven
*Walter the Baker* by Eric Carle

### Math

○ Provide pennies and five plastic counting jars. Write one numeral from 1-5 on each of five plastic jars. Cut slits in the tops of the jars to provide a drop slit for pennies. **Caution:** This is an adult-only step. Encourage the children to drop the number of pennies into the jar that corresponds with the number written on the outside of the jar.

✔ **Special Needs Adaptation:** This is a good time to work with money and to talk about the coins we use. Provide some pennies for the child to count. Place a nickel on a piece of construction paper and write the numeral 5 beside it in large print. Tell the child to put that many pennies next to the nickel.

### Science

○ Show the children what happens when you drop currants or raisins into a glass of clear carbonated drink. The raisins will rise up and down in the drink. The air bubbles in the drink surround the currant and lift it to the surface. At the surface, the air bubbles will pop and the currant will drop to the bottom of the glass. Point out that the movement of the currants is like the movement of an elevator going up and down.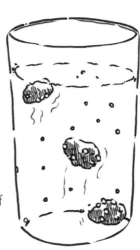

### Snack

○ Serve hot cross buns for snack. Discuss the buns. *Why are they called "hot cross buns?"*

### Writing

○ Print a sign that says, "Hot Cross Buns—1d." Explain that this means a hot cross bun costs one penny in England. Make a second sign that says, "Hot Cross Buns—1¢." Explain that this means the bun costs 1 penny in the United States. Provide paper, markers, and pencils and invite the children to copy the signs.

## Home Connection

○ Suggest that families serve hot cross buns for breakfast or for dessert.

# Fast Food

## adapted by Richele Bartkowiak and Pam Schiller

(Tune: A Ram Sam Sam)
A hamburger, a hamburger,
Pepperoni pizza
And a hamburger.
Lemonade, lemonade,
Pepperoni pizza
And a hamburger.
A chicken nugget,
A chicken nugget,
Crispy French fries
And a chicken nugget.

Chocolate shake,
Chocolate shake,
Crispy French fries
And a chicken nugget.
A tater tot, a tater tot,
Grilled cheese sandwich
And a tater tot.
Cherry slush, cherry slush,
Grilled cheese sandwich
And a tater tot.

## Vocabulary

cherry slush
chicken nugget
chocolate shake
French fries
grilled cheese sandwich
hamburger
lemonade
pepperoni pizza
tater tot

## Theme Connections

Health and Safety
Humor
Things I Like

# Did You Know?

○ Fast food is not a new idea. In ancient Rome, vendors sold food ready-to-eat from street stalls.

○ Frank Hardart and Joe Horn opened the first Automat on June 9, 1902—the beginnings of modern fast food.

○ The first drive-up McDonald's was opened in 1975. McDonald's introduced Chicken McNuggets in 1983.

○ There are 600 Kentucky Fried Chicken outlets in China, which is the second largest fast-food market after the United States.

○ About half of the calories in the average fast-food meal come from fat.

○ The gourmet food capital of the world is Paris, France, which is also home to McDonald's, Burger King, TGI Friday's, Pizza Hut, Chili's, and many other American fast-food restaurants.

# Literacy Links

### Oral Language

○ Discuss fast-food restaurants. Ask questions. *Where do you like to eat? Which meal is your favorite? Why?*

 **English Language Learner Strategy:** Use visual cues, gestures, and concrete objects when asking questions. Accept children's nonverbal responses.

### Print Awareness

○ Show the children items from fast-food restaurants. Are they able to read the names of the restaurants?

○ Write a new verse to the song incorporating some of the children's favorite fast foods.

# Curriculum Connections

### Art

○ Provide paint and easel paper. Encourage the children to paint fast food.

### Blocks

○ Encourage the children to build fast-food restaurants. Provide writing materials so they can label their restaurants.

### Dramatic Play

○ Fill the center with empty and clean fast-food cups, French fry holders, napkins, and so on. Encourage the children to set up the fast-food restaurant of their choice. Provide writing materials for the children to use to label their restaurant.

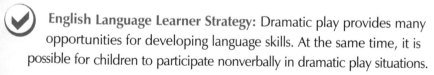 **English Language Learner Strategy:** Dramatic play provides many opportunities for developing language skills. At the same time, it is possible for children to participate nonverbally in dramatic play situations.

### Language

○ Invite the children to list the components of their favorite fast-food meals. List them on a sheet of paper and encourage the children to illustrate the components of their fast-food meals.

### Field Trip

○ Take a field trip to a local fast-food restaurant. Discuss the menu. *What's healthy? What's not?*

## Book Corner

**Special Needs Adaptation:** Before leaving on the field trip, talk to the child with special needs and tell him exactly where you are going and what will happen. Remind him of safety rules associated with field trips, such as never leaving with a stranger, asking for help, and looking both ways when crossing the street. Even though an adult will be with him on the field trip, reviewing these rules will increase the likelihood that the child will follow them.

### Math

○ Print one numeral from 1-5 on each of five empty, clean French fry cartons. Cut yellow foam into strips to represent French fries. Challenge the children to place the number of French fries in each carton designated by the number printed on the outside of the carton.

### Science

○ Provide photos of food. Encourage the children to sort the photos into healthy and unhealthy foods.

**Special Needs Adaptation:** Learning to make healthy food choices can be difficult for all children, especially those with cognitive disabilities. Many children with special needs develop health issues related to being overweight. Use this activity to reinforce which foods are healthy choices and which are not. Give the child two pieces of construction paper, one red and one green. Encourage her to sort the pictures of food by putting the healthy choices on the green paper and the unhealthy choices on the red paper.

### Social Studies

○ Discuss the environmental elements of fast-food containers. *Are they environmentally friendly?* Talk about what "environmentally friendly" means.

### Writing

○ Print the names of fast-food chains on chart paper and encourage the children to use magnetic letters to copy them.

# Home Connection

○ Encourage families to write a short story about the last time they ate fast food.

# Sippin' Cider Through a Straw

## Vocabulary

| | |
|---|---|
| cheek | prettiest |
| cider | sippin' |
| jaw | slip |
| lip | straw |
| moral | tale |
| pa | through |
| pail | |

## Theme Connections

Friends and Family
Humor

## Did You Know?

- In the United States, some companies use the term *cider* to refer to apple juice with no preservatives, and *juice* to refer to apple juice that has been pasteurized.
- It takes about 36 apples to create one gallon of apple cider.

The prettiest girl *(The prettiest girl)*
I ever saw *(I ever saw)*
Was sippin' ci- *(Was sippin' ci-)*
Der through a straw.
*(Der through a straw)*

The prettiest girl I ever saw
Was sippin' cider through a straw

I asked her if *(I asked her if)*
She'd show me how
*(She'd show me how)*
To sip that ci- *(To sip that ci-)*
Der through a straw.
*(Der through a straw)*

I asked her if she'd show me how
To sip that cider through a straw

First cheek to cheek
*(First cheek to cheek)*
Then jaw to jaw *(Then jaw to jaw)*
We sipped that ci-
*(We sipped that ci-)*
Der through a straw.
*(Der through a straw)*

First cheek to cheek and jaw to jaw,
We sipped that cider through a straw

Then suddenly *(Then suddenly)*
That straw did slip
*(That straw did slip)*
And we sipped ci-
*(And we sippped ci-)*
Der lip to lip. *(Der lip to lip)*

Then suddenly that straw did slip,
And we sipped cider lip to lip.

That's how I got *(That's how I got)*
My mother-in-law
*(My mother-in-law)*
And 49 kids *(And 49 kids)*
To call me Pa. *(To call me Pa)*

That's how I got my mother-in-law
And 49 kids to call me Pa.

The moral of *(The moral of)*
This little tale *(This little tale)*
Is sip your cider *(Is sip your cider)*
From a pail. *(From a pail)*

The moral of this little tale
Is sip your cider from a pail.

# Literacy Links

### Oral Language
❍ Teach the children the American Sign Language signs for *apple*, *boy*, and *girl* (page 116).

### Print Awareness
❍ Print *forty-nine* on chart paper. Print the numeral 49 just below it. Point out that there are two ways to write forty-nine—in words and in numerals.

# Curriculum Connections

### Art
❍ Provide art paper, tempera paint, and half a straw for each child. Place a small amount of tempera paint on each child's paper and encourage him to use his straw to blow the paint into a design.

### Construction
❍ Provide plastic straws and masking tape. Encourage the children to create a sculpture or a structure with the straws.

### Discovery
❍ Provide each child with a cup of water and three straws. Suggest that they try to drink the water with one straw, then two straws, and finally all three straws.

### Games
❍ Place a piece of masking tape down the center of a 6' table. Place a straw on each side of the line at one end of the table. Each child will need a partner. Encourage the partners to blow their straws, keeping the straw on their side of the table, from one end of the table to the other in a race with their partner.

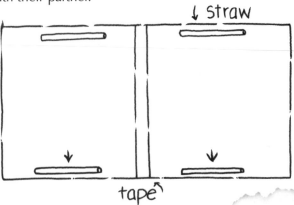

## Book Corner

### Gross Motor

○ Provide a pail and several straws. Use masking tape to make a toss line about three feet from the pail. Challenge the children to toss the straws into the pail.

 **Special Needs Adaptation:** For children with gross motor issues, make the toss line closer to the pail.

### Math

○ Give the children a straw and challenge them to find other things in the room that are exactly the same length as the straw.

○ Place 49 blocks or beads in a long line. Tell the children that the blocks represent the number of children in the song. Ask the children to walk the length of the blocks. If they are able to count, ask them to count to whatever number they can count to as they walk. Make a graph showing the number of children in each child's family.

○ Provide straws cut in 1", 2", 3", 4", 5", and 6" lengths. Encourage the children to sort the straws by length, and to create lines of straws arranged from the shortest to the tallest straw. Have them reverse the order and arrange the straws from the tallest to the shortest straw.

### Music and Movement

○ Demonstrate how to dance cheek to cheek. Play some music and encourage the children to select a partner and dance cheek to cheek.

 **English Language Learner Strategy:** Model the dance and stay nearby to provide assistance, if necessary.

### Snack

○ Make apple cider with the children using the recipe on page 101. Serve at snack time. Provide straws for drinking.

## Home Activities

○ Suggest that families serve apple cider for a treat.
○ Encourage the children to ask their parents or grandparents how they met.

# Apples and Bananas

I like to eat, eat, eat,
Apples and bananas.
I like to eat, eat, eat,
Apples and bananas.

I like to ate, ate, ate,
Aypuls and baynaynays.
I like to ate, ate, ate,
Aypuls and baynaynays.

I like to eet, eet, eet,
Eeples and beeneenees.
I like to eet, eet, eet,
Eeples and beeneenees.

I like to ite, ite, ite,
Iples and bininis.
I like to ite, ite, ite,
Iples and bininis.

I like to ote, ote, ote,
Oples and bononos.
I like to ote, ote, ote,
Oples and bononos.

I like to ute, ute, ute,
Upples and bununus.
I like to ute, ute, ute,
Upples and bununus.

I like to eat, eat, eat,
Apples and bananas.
I like to eat, eat, eat,
Apples and bananas.

## Vocabulary

apple
banana
eat

## Theme Connections

Health and Safety
Things I Like

## Did You Know?

○ Apples come in all shades of reds, greens, and yellows, and are a member of the rose family.

○ A medium apple has 80 calories. Apples are fat-, sodium-, and cholesterol-free, and are a great source of the fiber pectin.

○ Apples ripen six to ten times faster at room temperature than when refrigerated.

○ North America got its first taste of bananas in 1876 at the Philadelphia Centennial Exhibition. Each banana was wrapped in foil and sold for 10 cents.

○ Today, the average American consumes about 25 pounds a year of bananas, which are rich in potassium and vitamins A, B, and C.

○ See page 72 in "Go Bananas!" for more information about bananas.

# Literacy Links

### Letter Knowledge/Phonological Awareness

○ Print *apple* on chart paper. Print the word four more times, changing the beginning letter to another vowel as in the song. Read the list of words. Point out that the only letter change that happens is the change of the first letter and yet the word changes significantly. Do the same with *banana*. This time, several letters change. Are the children able to hear the vowel sounds change in each word?

### Oral Language

○ Discuss the differences between fruits and vegetables.

○ Collect a variety of fruits, such as an apple, banana, orange, and so on. Place one fruit in a paper bag. Invite a child to touch the fruit, describe it, and name it. Repeat with each fruit, discussing the characteristics of each.

○ Teach the children the American Sign Language signs for *apple* and *banana* (page 116).

○ Talk about apples. Make a Word Web. Print *apple* in the center of a sheet of chart paper. Draw a circle around the word. Encourage the children to tell you what they know about apples. Write their contributions on lines that extend out from the circle. Discuss bananas in the same way.

 **English Language Learner Strategy:** Provide pictures of things that are related to apples and let the children create a Word Web using the pictures.

# Curriculum Connections

### Art

○ Provide red, yellow, and green tempera paint. Encourage the children to paint pictures of apples and bananas.

○ Provide watercolors. Invite children to cover sheets of paper in red and yellow watercolors. When the paper is dry, ask the children to tear apple and banana shapes from the paper.

### Discovery

○ Invite the children to paint a sheet of paper the pink color of apple blossoms. Place their papers in a sunny location for several days. *What happens to the pink color?* Point out that most apple blossoms are pink when they first bloom but turn white as they fade in the sunshine.

## Fine Motor

○ Provide apple seeds and tweezers. Invite the children to pick up the seeds with the tweezers and move them onto a white or pale yellow paper plate to simulate apple seeds inside an apple.

## Games

○ Invite the children to play Fruit Basket Turn Over. Sit with the children in a circle. Select one child to stand in the center. Assign the name of a fruit to each child. The child in the center of the circle calls out the name of two fruits. The two children who are assigned the names of those fruits must quickly change seats. The child in the middle also tries to reach one of those two seats. The one left standing then calls the name of two other fruits. He or she may also call, "Fruit basket turnover," and everyone must change seats.

## Language

○ Encourage children to dictate recipes for their favorite apple or banana dish.

## Math

○ Tell the children it takes 36 apples to produce enough juice to make one gallon of apple juice. Provide 36 apples and an empty 1-gallon milk container. Have the children arrange the apples into six rows of six apples. Count the apples with them.

## Music and Movement

○ Play "Here We Go 'Round the Apple Tree" to the tune of "Mulberry Bush." Have the children hold hands and skip in a circle for the first verse and then act out the remaining verses.

**Here We Go 'Round the Apple Tree**
*Here we go round the apple tree,*
*The apple tree, the apple tree.*
*Here we go round the apple tree,*
*In the apple orchard.*

*This is the way we plant the seeds…in the apple orchard.*
*Now we watch the little seed sprouts…in the apple orchard.*
*Little seeds to apple trees grow…in the apple orchard.*
*Spring time will bring pink flowers…in the apple orchard.*
*At last the apples begin to grow…in the apple orchard.*
*Will you help us pick the apples…from the apple tree?*

# Shortnin' Bread

## Vocabulary

coffee
cover
dance
doctor
favorite
lid
popped up
shortnin' bread
sick
sing
skillet

## Theme Connections

Community Workers
Friends and Family
Things I Like

Put on the skillet, slip on the lid.
Mama's gonna make a little shortnin' bread.
That ain't all she's gonna do.
Mama's gonna make a little coffee, too.

Chorus:
Mama's little baby loves shortnin', shortnin',
Mama's little baby loves shortnin' bread.
Mama's little baby loves shortnin', shortnin',
Mama's little baby loves shortnin' bread.

Three little children lyin' in bed,
They were sick, covers over their heads.
Sent for the doctor and the doctor said,
"Give those children some shortnin' bread."

(Chorus)

When those children, sick in bed,
Heard that talk about shortnin' bread.
Popped up well to dance and sing,
'Cause shortnin' bread's their favorite thing.

(Chorus)

## Did You Know?

o  There is some confusion regarding the food referred to in this African-American folk song. Some food historians think it is Scottish shortbread. Others suggest the recipe was a simple quick bread (non-yeast) composed of flour (possibly cornmeal) and fat (probably lard). Which is correct? If the song refers to food typically eaten by 18th and 19th century African-Americans, it is most likely the cornmeal and lard mixture and not the Scottish-type shortbread, which uses granulated white sugar, pure creamery butter, and white flour, expensive materials in the 18th and 19th centuries.

o  Many historians believe that shortening bread was cornbread made with cooking fat. In the American South, shortcake and shortbread meant a combination of cornmeal and grease.

# Literacy Links

### Comprehension

○ Have the children say the rhyme, "Five Little Monkeys Jumping on the Bed." *Which parts of the rhyme are similar to things that are mentioned in "Shortnin' Bread"?*

**Five Little Monkeys Jumping on the Bed**
*Five little monkeys jumping on the bed.*
*One fell off and bumped her head.*
*Mama called the doctor, and the doctor said,*
*"No more monkeys jumping on the bed!"*
(Repeat, subtracting a monkey each time. You can say the rhyme using fingers or let children act it out.)

### Oral Language

○ Teach the children the American Sign Language signs for *mama* and *baby* (page 116).

○ Make a list of children's favorite foods. Sing the song, filling in other favorite foods listed by the children. For example, "Mama's little baby loves pizza, pizza. Mama's little baby loves pizza pie."

# Curriculum Connections

### Cooking

○ Make shortening bread with the class using one of the following recipes.
*Scottish Shortbread:* Preheat an oven or a toaster oven to 325 degrees. Cream 1 cup butter in a large bowl. Sift 2 cups all purpose flour, ½ cup confectioners' sugar, and ¼ teaspoon salt in a second bowl. Gradually add the dry ingredients to the butter and mix thoroughly. Press the mixture into an ungreased 9" x 9" pan. Press the edges down. Prick every half-inch with a fork around the sides, and then work your way to the center. Mark into twenty squares, cutting halfway through the dough. Bake 25 to 30 minutes. Shortbread should not be brown. Cool in the pan and cut while warm. When cool, let the children decorate their shortbread with frosting, chocolate chips, coconut, and so on.

## Book Corner

*Five Little Monkeys Bake a Birthday Cake* by Eileen Christelow
*Five Little Monkeys Jumping on the Bed* by Eileen Christelow
*Hush, Little Baby* by Shari Halpren

*Cornbread:* Ingredients: 2 tablespoons baking powder, ½ cup vegetable oil, 2 cups buttermilk, 3 eggs, ½ cup honey or sugar, 1 teaspoon salt, 1 cup whole wheat flour, and 3 cups yellow cornmeal. Mix dry ingredients together and separately add wet ingredients together. Stir dry and wet mixtures together until the dry ingredients are moistened. Pour mixture into a greased pan, muffin tins, or iron skillet. Cook for 25 minutes at 350 degrees.

### Dramatic Play

○ Provide cups, spoons, bowls, and pans. Encourage the children to role-play the song. Be sure to provide a bag for the doctor and a blanket for the bed.

### Field Trip

○ Visit a bakery where bread is baked on the premises. Make a list of the different types of bread you see.

### Math

○ Provide baking cups and muffin tins. Encourage the children to match one paper to each crate in the muffin tin. If the baking cups are different colors, suggest that the children create patterns in the muffin tins.

### Music and Movement

○ Challenge the children to make up a dance to the song. For example, they may skip in a circle, lock arms and skip in a circle, clap their hands and shake their hips, and so on.

### Social Studies

○ Discuss the origin of shortening bread, and then show the children the location of Scotland on a globe or on a world map, and the portion of the United States known as the South.

### Writing

○ Print *mama* and *baby* on large index cards. Encourage the children to copy the words with magnetic letters.

# Home Connection

○ Encourage children to talk with their families about things that make them feel better when they are sick. Some people like fruit, others like chicken soup. What else makes the list?

# A Peanut Sat on a Railroad Track

Peanut sat on a railroad track,
His heart was all a-flutter,
Round the bend came number ten.
Toot! Toot! Peanut butter!
SQUISH!

## Vocabulary

bend
flutter
heart
number ten
peanut
railroad
squish
ten
toot

## Theme Connections

Humor
Transportation

## Did You Know?

○ The first trains were hauled by rope or pulled by horses. Beginning in the early 19th century almost all trains were powered by a steam engine locomotive. From the 1920s onward, they began to be replaced by less labor-intensive and cleaner diesel and electric locomotives. At the same time, self-propelled multiple-unit diesel and electric vehicles became more common in passenger service.

○ Most countries had replaced steam locomotives for day-to-day use by the 1970s. A few countries—most notably China where coal is cheap and in plentiful supply—still use steam locomotives. Historical steam trains still run in many other countries for the leisure market and for train enthusiasts.

○ Locomotives weigh between 400,000 to 540,000 pounds.

○ See information about peanuts in "Peanut Butter" on page 17 and "Goober Peas" on page 44.

## Literacy Links

### Oral Language

○ Talk about trains. Name the cars on the train. Ask questions. *Have you seen a train? Where? What color was the engine? What color was the caboose? Have you ridden on a train? Where did you go?*

○ Provide photos of Holstein cows, easel paper, and black and white tempera paint. Encourage the children to create a black-and-white design to resemble the hide of the Holstein cow.

## Blocks

○ Build a diary farm. Provide green fabric to use as a ground cover of grass, boxes of various shapes to make milking barns and milk tanks, plastic dairy cows, and other related materials. *Where is the milk stored? Where is the food to feed the cows stored?*

## Discovery

○ Place several products that come from milk on the table; for example, cheese, yogurt, and butter. Invite the children to have a tasting party. *Which milk product do you like best?* **Allergy Warning:** Make sure none of the children have dairy allergies or are lactose intolerant before allowing them to taste dairy products.

## Dramatic Play

○ Fill a latex glove half full with a mixture of white tempera paint and water. Make a knot in the open end to tie the glove closed. Use a straight pin to poke two or three small holes in the tips of the fingers of the glove. Allow children to squeeze the finger to simulate milking a cow. Encourage them to sing a milking song to the tune of "Here We Go 'Round the Mulberry Bush."

> ### This Is the Way We Milk the Cows
> *This is the way we milk the cows,*
> *Milk the cows, milk the cows.*
> *This is the way we milk the cows*
> *So early in the morning*

## Fine Motor

○ Make a copy of the cow pattern (page 115). Glue the copy to the top of a box with a lid (stationery-box size). Cut a 1" hole next to the mouth of the cow. Provide tweezers and unpopped popcorn kernels. Invite the children to use the tweezers to pick up the corn and feed it to the cow by dropping it through the hole in the box. When finished, feed the corn to squirrels or other animals, or wash the corn and pop it for snack.

○ Copy the cow pattern (page 115). Laminate the cow and glue a strip of magnetic tape to its back. Turn a large copy-paper size box upside down. On the bottom of the box, use a marker to draw a pathway that begins in a pasture and moves to a barn. Cut out one side of the box. Place the cow by the pasture. Have the children hold a magnet in one hand and place it through the open side of the box to move the cow from the pasture to the barn.

## Book Corner

### Listening

❍ Provide squirt bottles of water and a tin pail. Invite the children to squirt water into the pail to simulate the sound of the cow's milk hitting a pail.

### Math

❍ Make five (or more) copies of the cow pattern on page 115. Draw one spot on the first cow, two spots on the second cow, and so on until you have five spots on the fifth cow. If children are ready, use higher numbers. Provide the plastic numerals 1-5 and encourage the children to match the numerals to the spots.

 **Special Needs Adaptation:** Use black checkers for the spots. They are easy to pick up and to manipulate.

### Music and Movement

❍ Teach the children "My Cow May" to the tune of "Five Little Ducks."

**My Cow May**
*I have a cow and her name is May,*
*She loves to feast on corn and hay.*
*She moos and moos and swishes her tail,*
*And gives me milk in my pail, pail, pail.*
*Drip-drop, plip-plop, drip-drop.*
*Drip-drop, plip-plop, drip-drop.*

### Science

❍ Invite the children to plant rye grass seed for the cows to eat.

### Social Studies

❍ Make butter with the children (page 105). Give each child a small plastic baby food jar filled with two tablespoons of whipping cream at room temperature. Encourage the children to shake the containers until the cream thickens into butter. Spread on crackers or bread and eat.

## Home Connection

❍ Encourage families to help their children make a list of milk-related products in their homes.

# Chocolate Chip Cookies

## Vocabulary

butter
chew
chocolate chip
clean
cookie
crumbs
door
eat
flour
halo
harp
magic
oven
plate
power
quarter hour
sing
store
sugar
wing

## Theme Connections

Counting
Things I Like

(Tune: Mary Had a Little Lamb)
Chorus:
Chocolate chip cookies, you gotta have more.
You can bake 'em in the oven, or buy 'em at the store.
But whatever you do, have 'em ready at my door
And I'll love you till I die.

They're made out of sugar and butter and flour.
You can put 'em in the oven about a quarter hour.
But the thing that gives them their magic power
Is the chocolate chips inside.

(Chorus)

You can't eat one, you can't eat two.
Once you start chewing, there's nothing to do.
But clean your plate, and eat the crumbs too.
Then go and find some more.

(Chorus)

Now when I die, I don't want wings
A golden halo or a harp that sings.
Give me a book, and someone that brings me
Chocolate chip cookies all day.

(Chorus)

## Did You Know?

○ The original chocolate chip cookie, the Toll House Cookie, was invented by Ruth Graves Wakefield in 1930. Ruth and her husband Kenneth owned the Toll House Inn, on the outskirts of Whitman, Massachusetts. Ruth cooked homemade meals for her guests; one day, she had to substitute semi-sweet chocolate for baker's chocolate in a cookie recipe. She chopped the chocolate in bits, and when she took the cookies from

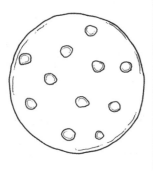

the oven, the semi-sweet chocolate had not melted into the dough like the baker's chocolate did. These cookies with chocolate "chips" were an immediate hit with her guests.

❍ The official state cookie of Massachusetts is the chocolate chip cookie.

❍ On February 7, 2001, the chocolate chip cookie was declared the official cookie of the Commonwealth of Pennsylvania.

# Literacy Links

### Letter Knowledge/Phonological Awareness

❍ Print *chocolate chip cookies* on chart paper. Ask the children to identify the first letter of each word. Point out that the first two words, *chocolate chip*, are called *alliterative* because the words start with the same sound. *Does anyone have a name that begins with the letters Ch?*

### Oral Language

❍ Teach the children the American Sign Language sign for *cookie* (page 116).

❍ Encourage the children to discuss and describe their favorite cookies.

### Phonological Awareness

❍ Ask the children to say the following tongue twister: *Choosey children eat chocolate chip cookies.* Write the tongue twister on chart paper. Underline each word that begins with /ch/. Point out that this is an example of *alliteration*.

# Curriculum Connections

### Art

❍ Give each child a small 6" paper plate. Provide brown tempera paint, brown crayons, and brown glue (glue with dark brown or black tempera paint mixed in) in squeeze bottles. Have the children paint or color their plate to look like a cookie. Encourage them to use the glue to add "chocolate chips" to their cookies.

### Cooking

❍ Invite children to help you make the most famous chocolate chip cookie—the Toll House Cookie. Follow the recipe on the back of the chocolate chip package.

### Dramatic Play

O Provide props for a cookie store; for example, cookie trays, pretend cookies, aprons, cash register, bags, tongs, and so on. Help the children label the trays of cookies.

### Field Trip

O Take a trip to a bakery and look for chocolate chip cookies. *How many different kinds of cookies do you find?*

### Language

O Use cookie boxes to make puzzles. Cut the front panel from the box. Laminate it and then cut it into puzzle pieces.

### Math

O Paint four cardboard pizza trays to look like chocolate chip cookies. Cut one tray into eighths, one into fourths, one into thirds, and one in half. Give these cookie puzzles to the children and challenge them to take them apart and put them back together. Talk with them as they work. Use fraction terms; for example, *fourths, halves, eighths,* and *thirds.*

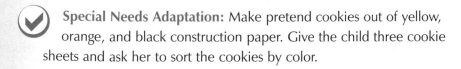 **Special Needs Adaptation:** Make pretend cookies out of yellow, orange, and black construction paper. Give the child three cookie sheets and ask her to sort the cookies by color.

O Make a Chocolate Chip Cookie Numeral Matching game by coloring small paper plates brown for cookies and using brown or black glue to add "chocolate chips" to the cookies. Make 1-5 chips (or higher numbers if children are ready) on each of five cookies. Provide numerals and have the children label each cookie with a numeral that matches the number of chips on the cookie. After the children match the cookies and numerals, have them close their eyes and attempt to count the "chips" on each cookie by touching the cookies and feeling for the "chips."

### Writing

O Provide empty cookie bags or boxes. Encourage the children to use magnetic letters to copy the names of the cookies. For younger children, provide two of each package and ask children to match the packages.

## Home Connection

O Encourage the children to interview each family member about his or her favorite kind of cookie.

*The Chocolate Chip Cookie Contest* by Barbara Douglass
*Cookie Count: A Tasty Pop-Up* by Robert Sabuda
*The Doorbell Rang* by Pat Hutchins
*If You Give a Mouse a Cookie* by Laura Joffe Numeroff

SONGS AND ACTIVITIES

# Betty Botter

Betty Botter bought some butter,
"But," she said, "The butter's bitter.
If I put it in my batter,
It will make my batter bitter.
But a bit of better butter,
That would make my batter better."
So she bought a bit of butter,
Better than her bitter butter.
And she put it in her batter,
And the batter wasn't bitter.
So 'twas better Betty Botter
Bought a bit of better butter.

## Vocabulary

batter
bit
bitter
bought
butter

## Theme Connections

Farms
Things I Like

## Did You Know?

○ Butter is a dairy product made by churning fresh cream until it forms into butter. It consists of an emulsion of water and milk proteins in a matrix of more than 80% fat. It is used as a condiment as well as for cooking, in much the same way as vegetable oils or lard.

○ Butter is generally pale yellow, but can vary from deep yellow to nearly white. Butter is typically paler when dairy cattle feed on stored hay rather than on fresh grass in the winter. In countries where cows eat grass year-round, butter seldom changes color.

○ There are many types of butter—salted, unsalted, semi-salted, whipped, and cultured. Butter sold in United States markets is typically salted.

○ Salted butter can be kept at room temperature for two to three days in warm weather or for up to ten weeks in the refrigerator. Unsalted butter can be kept in the refrigerator for six weeks. Butter can be kept in the freezer for up to six months, but may lose a bit of its flavor.

## Literacy Links

### Letter Knowledge

○ Print *botter*, *batter*, *bitter*, and *butter* on chart paper. Ask the children to find the letter in each word that is different.

 **Special Needs Adaptation:** Adapt this activity by focusing on the letter "b". Remind the child that *butter* starts with the same letter *banana* starts with. Make a list with the child of other words that start with the letter "b".

## Phonological Awareness

○ Print this tongue twister on chart paper. Encourage the children to help you locate all the words that begin with the letter "b". Pont out that the repetition of a beginning letter sound in several words in a row is called *alliteration*. Have the children say the tongue twister with you slowly. *What sound is repeated over and over?*

# Curriculum Connections

## Art

○ Provide several shades of yellow tempera paint, paper, and paintbrushes, and invite the children to explore the many hues of butter with paint and paper.

## Dramatic Play

○ Provide kitchen props, including pots, pans, mixing bowl, spoons, and so on. Invite the children to pretend to mix Betty Botter's batter.

 **English Language Learner Strategy:** Dramatic play provides many opportunities for developing language skills. At the same time, it is possible for children to participate nonverbally in dramatic play situations.

## Fine Motor

○ Provide yellow playdough. Encourage the children to shape the yellow playdough into sticks of butter.

## Language

○ Provide kitchen tools, such as a funnel, sifter, strainer, whip, measuring cups, measuring spoons, spatula, and so on. Have the children sort the tools by how they are used.

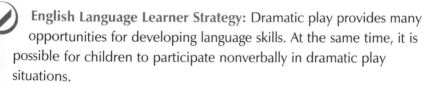

 **Special Needs Adaptation:** As the child sorts the tools, ask him to describe each tool to you. You may have to tell him how it is used, but he can help you describe it such as *flat, round, smooth, sharp,* and so on.

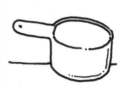

## Book Corner

### Math

○ Fill empty butter boxes or margarine tubs with clay. Put a different amount of clay different in each container so the weight of each is different. Challenge the children to arrange the boxes or tubs from lightest to heaviest.

### Music and Movement

○ Discuss the feel of butter when it is soft. Have the children remove their shoes but not their socks. Play music and encourage them to pretend that they are slipping and sliding in melted butter.

### Social Studies

○ Make butter with the children. Give each child a small plastic baby food jar filled with two tablespoons whipping cream at room temperature. Encourage the children to shake the containers until the cream thickens into butter. You may want to add a pinch of salt before spreading on crackers or bread to eat.

### Writing

○ Print *butter*, *batter*, and *bitter* on chart paper. Provide magnetic letters and encourage the children to copy the words.

# Home Connection

○ Encourage children to discuss butter with their families. Do they use butter or margarine? Do they use both margarine and butter? What is their preference and why?

# My Lollipop  by Pam Schiller

## Vocabulary

lollipop
my
own
stop
tongue
yours

## Theme Connections

Counting
Friends and Family
Opposites
Things I Like

(Tune: One Bottle of Pop)
One lollipop, two lollipops,
Three lollipops, four lollipops,
Five lollipops, six lollipops,
Seven lollipops, stop!

Don't stick your tongue on my lollipop,
My lollipop, my lollipop.
Don't stick your tongue on my lollipop.
Go get your own!

My lollipop is my lollipop,
My lollipop, my lollipop.
My lollipop is my lollipop,
Go get your own!

My lollipop, your lollipop,
My lollipop, your lollipop,
My lollipop, your lollipop,
Lolli lollipop STOP!

## Did You Know?

○ Lollipops are lumps of hard candy on the end of a stick.
○ Lollipops come in all shapes and sizes. The most popular brands are Charms Lollipops and Tootsie Pops.
○ According to the National Confectionary Association, the first candy on a stick was created by cavemen who maintained beehives and collected honey by stick. Not wanting to waste the sweet residue, they likely licked the utensil, and thus the first unintentional lollipop or candy on a stick was born.
○ See page 20 in "Have You Been to Candyland?" for more candy facts.

# Literacy Links

### Letter Knowledge
○ Print *lollipop* on chart paper. Have the children count the number of times each letter shows up in the word.

### Oral Language
○ Teach the children the America Sign Language sign for *lollipop* (page 116).

### Oral Language/Print Awareness
○ Discuss lollipops. Which flavor of lollipop does each child like best? Make a list of all the colors lollipops come in. Make a list of flavors. Which color or flavor is the most popular?

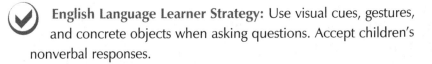 **English Language Learner Strategy:** Use visual cues, gestures, and concrete objects when asking questions. Accept children's nonverbal responses.

### Segmentation
○ Clap the syllables in *lollipop*. Do any of the children have a name that has the same number of syllables as *lollipop*?

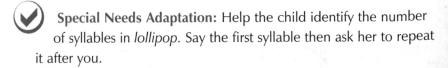 **Special Needs Adaptation:** Help the child identify the number of syllables in *lollipop*. Say the first syllable then ask her to repeat it after you.

# Curriculum Connections

### Art
○ Provide bright colors of tempera paint, easel paper, and paintbrushes. Invite the children to paint lollipops.

### Construction
○ Provide paper plates, crayons, yarn, construction paper, and tongue depressors or craft sticks. Encourage the children to draw faces on their paper plates. Have them cut or tear tongues from red construction paper and glue them to their faces. Suggest that they glue their faces to tongue depressors to make puppets.

### Dramatic Play

○ Provide props to set up a pretend candy store; for example, candy containers (such as empty bags and boxes), lollipops made from construction paper and craft sticks, cash register, play money, and so on. Encourage the children to pretend to operate a candy store. Help them label their products.

### Field Trip

○ Visit a candy store. *What kind of lollipops do you see? What colors of lollipops do you see?*

### Language

○ Encourage children to finish the sentence "My favorite lollipop is …". Write their descriptions in sentence form on a piece of drawing paper and invite them to illustrate their sentences.

### Math

○ Make 15 lollipops by cutting circles from poster board, decorating them in bright colors, and gluing them to craft sticks. Write one numeral from 1-5 on each of five large plastic cups. Encourage the children to count the number of lollipops into the cups that match the numeral printed on the outside.

○ Make colorful lollipops by cutting circles from construction paper and gluing them to craft sticks, or use real lollipops. Give the children the lollipops and encourage them to sort them by color. Challenge them to line up the lollipops in a pattern; for example, two red lollipops, one yellow lollipop, two red lollipops, and so on.

 **Special Needs Adaptation:** Use two solid color lollipops only. The child can sort them by color and count the lollipops.

### Music and Movement

○ Invite the children to dance and sing along with "The Good Ship Lollipop."

### Snack

○ Provide lollipops for the children after they have had snack and encourage them to choose their favorite flavor. Graph the results.

SONGS AND ACTIVITIES

# Home Connection

○ Encourage the children to teach their families "My Lollipop."

# Who Took the Cookies From the Cookie Jar?

One, two, one, two, three, four!
*(Repeat the following motions while saying the chant below: clap hands, clap thighs, clap hands, clap thighs.)*
Who took the cookies from the cookie jar?
Evan took the cookies from the cookie jar.
Who me?
Yes, you.
Couldn't be.
Then who?
Madison took the cookies from the cookie jar.
Who me?
Yes, you.
Couldn't be.
Then who?

*(Continue the chant with Abbey, Austin, Gabrielle, or names of children in the group; end with Daddy)*

Daddy took the cookies from the cookie jar.
That's who!

✓ **Special Needs Adaptation:** Learning to use pronouns such as *my, yours, his,* and *hers* is often difficult for children with special needs. Use this song to talk about *yours/mine, his/her, me/you,* and so on.

## Vocabulary

cookie
cookie jar
you
me
who

## Theme Connections

Friends and Family
Humor

## Did You Know?

○ In the United States, a cookie is a small, flat baked cake. Its name comes from the Dutch word *koek'e* which means "little cake." Cookies were first made from little pieces of cake batter that were cooked separately in order to test oven temperature.
○ Cookies can be baked until crisp or just long enough that they stay soft, depending on the type of cookie. Cookies are made in a vast variety of styles, using a large array of ingredients including sugars, spices, chocolates, butter, peanut butter, nuts, and dried fruits.
○ Cookies are broadly classified according to how they are formed.
○ See page 85 in "Chocolate Chip Cookies" for more information about cookies.

# Literacy Links

### Comprehension

○ Make story characters for "The Runaway Cookie" (on page 100) using the animal patterns in the appendix on pages 113-115. Make copies of the patterns, color them, and then laminate them. Glue the animal characters onto tongue depressors.

### Oral Language

○ Discuss cookie jars. *Does everyone have a cookie jar? What other containers are used to hold cookies?* For example, tins, boxes, and plastic bags. Make a list of all the ways the children have seen cookies stored.

○ Teach children the American Sign Language sign for *cookie* (page 116).

○ Challenge the children to think of descriptive words to describe cookies; for example, *yummy, crumbly, crispy, tasty, delicious, warm,* and so on.

# Curriculum Connections

### Cooking

○ Make this no-cook recipe for Orange Ball Cookies with the children. Crush 35 vanilla wafers and place in a mixing bowl. Add ¼ cup orange juice and 2 tablespoons granulated sugar; mix well. Roll into balls and then roll in powdered sugar.

 **English Language Learner Strategy:** Create a rebus for this recipe (examples of rebus recipes on pages 103-109) to make it easier for the child to follow the directions.

### Discovery

○ Cut cookie shapes of squares, rectangles, ovals, circles, and diamonds from poster board. Challenge children to try to roll each type of cookie. *Which cookies roll? Which cookies do not roll?*

### Dramatic Play

○ Provide props for cookie baking; for example, playdough, cookie cutters, rolling pins, cookie trays, mixing bowls, and so on.

### Games

○ Hide poster board cutouts of cookies or plastic cookies in the room. Invite the children to find them. You may want to make additional copies of the cookie patterns (page 114) for this game.

## Book Corner

✔ **Special Needs Adaptation:** Looking for the hidden cookies will be easier if you offer verbal cues as to where to look. The first time the child plays the game, hide the cookie in plain view so he can find it easily.

○ Play Drop the Cookie in the Cookie Jar as you would play Drop the Clothespin. Cut cookies from poster board or use plastic cookies, if available. Have the children hold the cookie chest high, stand over the cookie jar, and then drop the cookie. Does it land in the jar?

✔ **Special Needs Adaptation:** Use a larger object, such as a bucket, for the cookie jar. Write cookie jar on it. Instead of poster board cookies, use larger objects, such as the lids from whipped topping container, which are easier to hold.

### Language
○ Give the children the story puppets from "The Runaway Cookies." Encourage them to retell the story.

### Language/Fine Motor
○ Cut poster board into a variety of shapes and sizes to represent a variety of cookies. Use glue to create chips (drops of glue) on a chocolate chip cookie and lines on a wafer cookie. Be sure the glue is dry before placing the cookies inside a cookie jar. Challenge children to place their hand inside the cookie jar and, without looking, identify the chocolate chip cookie, the wafer cookie, the largest cookie, the smallest cookie and so on.

### Math
○ Provide playdough, cookie cutters, and cookie trays. Encourage the children to cut out cookie shapes and place them in a pattern on the cookie tray.

### Snack
○ Serve a variety of small cookies for snack, for example, sandwich, cake, iced, wafer, and so on. Encourage the children to describe their favorite cookie.

# Home Connection

○ Ask children to look for a cookie jar at home. Who has one?

# More Learning and Fun

## Songs

### The Ants Go Marching

The ants go marching one by one,
Hurrah, hurrah.
The ants go marching one by one,
Hurrah, hurrah.
The ants go marching one by one,
The little one stops to suck his thumb.
And they all go marching down
To the ground
To get out
Of the rain.
BOOM! BOOM! BOOM! BOOM!

… two… tie her shoe…
… three… climb a tree…
… four… shut the door…
… five… take a dive…

### Clickety Clack
**(Tune: Mary Had a Little Lamb)**
Clickity, clackity, clickity clack!
The train speeds over the railroad track.
It rolls and rattles and screeches its song,
And pulls and jiggles its
Freight cars along.

Clickity, clackity, clickity, clack!
The engine in front is big and black.
The cars are filled with lots of things
Like milk, or oil, or mattress springs.

Clickity, clackity, clickity, clack!
The engineer waves, and I wave back.
I count the cars as the freight train goes,
And the whistle blows and blows,
And blows!

### It's Raining, It's Pouring
*(additional verse by Richele Bartkowiak)*
It's raining, it's pouring
The old man is snoring.
He bumped his head
When he went to bed,
And he couldn't get up in the morning.

It's raining, it's pouring
Playing inside is boring.
We want sunshine
And bright blue skies;
Don't make us wait till morning.

### Rain, Rain, Go Away
*(second verse by Pam Schiller)*
Rain, rain, go away.
Rain, rain, come back soon.
Little children want to play.
Little flowers want to bloom.

### Shiny Apples
**(Tune: Are You Sleeping?)**
Shiny apples, shiny apples
In a tree, in a tree,
Put one in my basket,
Put more in my basket
One, two, three
Apples for me!

# Chants

### Everywhere We Go
Everywhere we go
People want to know
Who we are
And where we come from,
So we tell them
We're from _____
Cool, cool _____
Wacky, wacky _____,
And if they don't hear us
We shout a little louder.
*(Repeat)*

Everywhere we go
People want to know
Who we are
And where we come from,
So we tell them
We're from _____
Neat, neat _____
Splendid, splendid _____
And if they don't hear us
We shout a little louder.

### Sound Off
Chorus:
Leader: Sound off
Group: 1 — 2
Leader: Sound off
Group: 3 — 4
Leader: Cadence count
Everyone: 1 — 2 — 3 — 4, 1 — 2 —— 3 — 4

Boys and girls they love to play.
They turn cartwheels every day.

(Chorus)

I'm so hungry—I want lunch—
Give me something good to crunch.

(Chorus)

Continue to make up verses.

# Fingerplays

### Apples Here and Apples There
Apples here, *(point to floor at your feet)*
Apples there, *(point away)*
Apples growing everywhere. *(hands overhead and spread)*
Some are high, *(point up)*
Some are low, *(point down)*
Apples everywhere we go. *(turn a circle)*
Apples to our left, *(extend left arm)*
Apples to our right, *(extend right arm)*
Apples, apples, day and night. *(clap hands together)*

### Apple Tree
This is the tree with leaves so green. *(stretch out fingers)*
Here are the apples that hang in-between. *(make fists with both hands)*
When the wind blows the apples will fall, *(blow and then swoop hands downward)*
Here is the basket to gather them all. *(form a basket with arms)*

### Little Red Apple
**(Tune: Twinkle, Twinkle Little Star)**
Way up high in the apple tree *(stretch arms up high)*
Two red apples smiled at me *(hold up two fingers)*
I shook that tree as hard as I could *(shake hands)*
Down came the apples, *(float hands downward)*
Mmmm—mmmm good! *(smile and rub stomach)*

### Little Red Apple
A little red apple grew high in a tree. *(point up)*
I looked up at it. *(shade eyes and look up)*
It looked down at me. *(shade eyes and look down)*
"Come down, please," I called. *(point down)*

# Banana Smoothie Rebus

(Using a rebus makes it easier for English language learners to follow directions.)

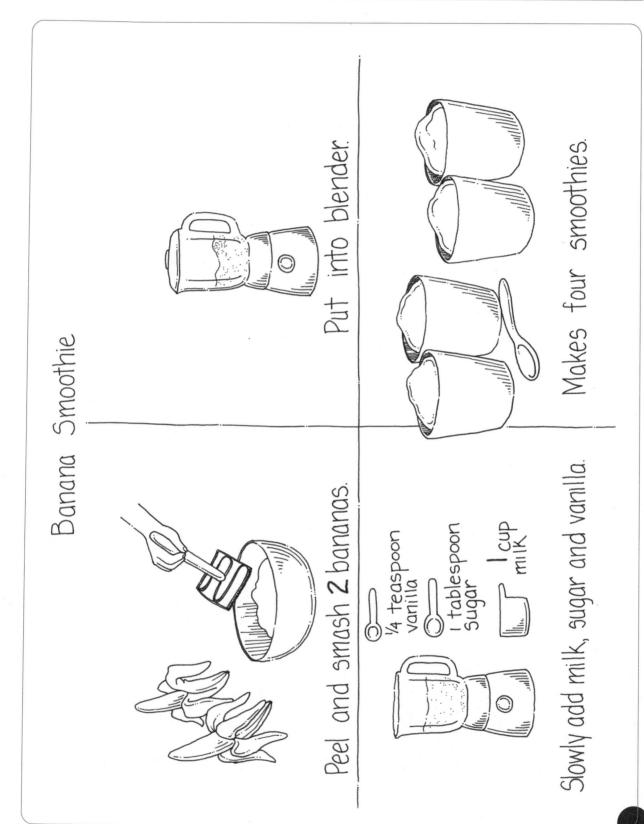

Banana Smoothie

Peel and smash **2** bananas.

¼ teaspoon vanilla

I tablespoon sugar

I cup milk

Slowly add milk, sugar and vanilla.

Put into blender.

Makes four smoothies.

# Lemonade Rebus

(Using a rebus makes it easier for English language learners to follow directions.)

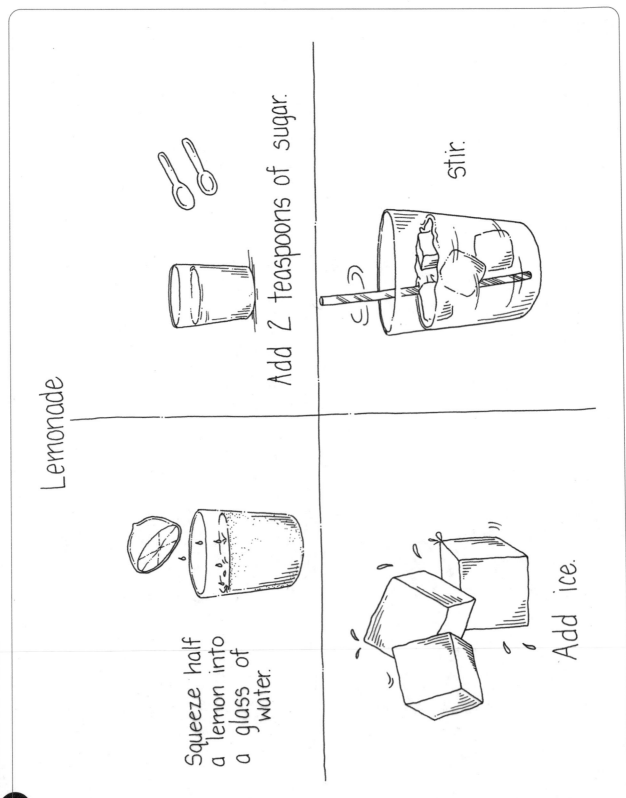

Lemonade

Squeeze half a lemon into a glass of water.

Add 2 teaspoons of sugar.

Stir.

Add ice.

# Purple Cow Shake Rebus

(Using a rebus makes it easier for English language learners to follow directions.)

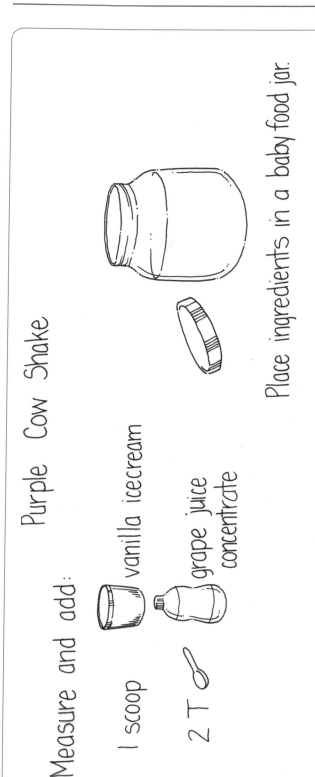

Purple Cow Shake

Measure and add:

1 scoop — vanilla icecream

2 T — grape juice concentrate

Place ingredients in a baby food jar.

Shake it!

Add a straw and drink.

# Trail Mix Rebus

(Using a rebus makes it easier for English language learners to follow directions.)

Trail Mix

5 5 5 5

Count 5 marshmallows, 5 pretzels, 5 pieces of cereal, and 5 peanuts.

Put into a plastic cup.

Enjoy!

# Watermelon Smoothie Rebus

(Using a rebus makes it easier for English language learners to follow directions.)

## Watermelon Smoothies

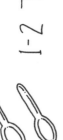  1-2 T Sugar

 ½ t Ground Ginger

 ⅛ t Almond Extract

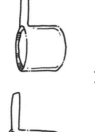  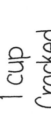

2 cups 1 cup ½ cup
Seedless Cracked Plain
Watermelon Ice Yogurt

Combine all ingredients in blender. Blend until smooth.

Makes 2-3 yummy servings.

# Sequence Cards

Making a peanut butter and jelly sandwich.

## Peanut Butter and Jelly Sandwich

Spread jelly on bread.

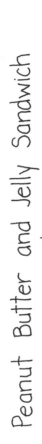

Spread peanut butter on bread.

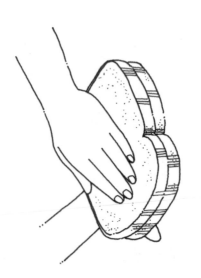

Eat!

Put bread together.

# Sequence Cards
Seed to Fruit

# Matching Game
Things That Go Together

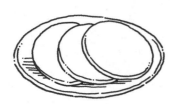

# Patterns

# Patterns

# Patterns

# American Sign Language Signs

Chew

Hamburger

Yes

Boy

Girl

Banana

Drink

Sandwich

Baby

Cow

Mama

Apple

Cookie

Lollipop

# References and Bibliography

Bulloch, K. 2003. *The mystery of modifying: Creative solutions.* Huntsville, TX: Education Service Center, Region VI.

Cavallaro, C. & M. Haney. 1999. *Preschool inclusion.* Baltimore, MD: Paul H. Brookes Publishing Company.

Gray, T. and S. Fleischman. Dec. 2004-Jan. 2005. "Research matters: Successful strategies for English language learners." *Educational Leadership,* 62, 84-85.

Hanniford, C. 1995. *Smart moves: Why learning is not all in your head.* Arlington, VA: Great Ocean Publications, p. 146.

Keller, M. 2004. "Warm weather boosts mood, broadens the mind." *Post Doctoral Study: The University of Michigan,* Anne Arbor, MI.

LeDoux, J. 1993. "Emotional memory systems in the brain." *Behavioral and Brain Research,* 58.

# Theme Index

# Children's Book Index

# Index

# The Complete Resource Book for Infants
## Over 700 Experiences for Children from Birth to 18 Months

*Pam Schiller*

The third in the best-selling series, *The Complete Resource Book for Infants* features over 700 experiences and activities that are perfect for infants from birth through 18 months. The experiences are organized by developmental area: language, social-emotional, physical, and cognitive, which are the essential building blocks for infant development. The appendix is chock-full of songs, rhymes, recipes, sign language, a developmental checklist, recommended books and toys, and family connection resources. 272 pages. 2005.

**Gryphon House / 19223 / Paperback**

# The Complete Resource Book for Toddlers and Twos
## Over 2000 Experiences and Ideas

*Pam Schiller*

Best-selling author Pam Schiller offers learning experiences that focus on the fertile areas of development for toddlers and twos. Easy to implement, each of the 100 daily topics is divided into activities and experiences that support language enrichment, cognitive development, social-emotional development, and physical development. Teachers will be delighted to add the ideas in this generous resource to their current lesson plans. 576 pages. 2003.

**Gryphon House / 16927 / Paperback**

# The Complete Resource Book for Preschoolers

*Pam Schiller and Kay Hastings*

*The Complete Resource Book* is an absolute must-have book for every teacher. Offering a complete plan for every day of the year, this is an excellent reference book for responding to children's specific interests. Each daily plan contains circle time activities, music and movement activities, suggested books, and six learning center ideas. The appendix, jam-packed with songs, recipes, and games, is almost a book in itself. *The Complete Resource Book* is like having a master teacher working at your side, offering you guidance and inspiration all year long. 463 pages. 1998.

**Gryphon House / 15327 / Paperback**

# The Complete Book and CD of Rhymes, Songs, Poems, Fingerplays and Chants

*Jackie Silberg and Pam Schiller, with Arrangements by Max Berry and Michael Oshiver*
This best-selling book now comes with a double CD featuring 50 songs! With songs such as "The More We Get Together" and "Make New Friends," children will sing and learn—all while having fun. Available July 2006.
**Gryphon House / Book and CD Combination /18492**

# Music from The Complete Book of Rhymes, Songs, Poems, Fingerplays and Chants

*Jackie Silberg, with Arrangements by Max Berry and Michael Oshiver*
The CD you've been waiting for is finally here! The companion to the best-selling book, this double CD features 50 songs to keep children singing and learning all year long with popular songs such as "The More We Get Together" and "Make New Friends." Available July 2006.
**Gryphon House / CD Only / 12078**

# The Complete Book of Activities, Games, Stories, Props, Recipes, and Dances
## For Young Children

*Pam Schiller and Jackie Silberg*

Are you searching for just the right story to reinforce your theme? Trying to play a game but can't remember the rules? Looking for your favorite no-bake cookie recipe? It's all right here! This book is chock-full of over 600 ways to enhance any curriculum. The companion to *The Complete Book of Rhymes, Songs, Poems, Fingerplays, and Chants,* it's a teacher's best friend! 512 pages. 2003.
★ Parent's Guide to Children's Media Award
★ Reader's Preference Editors Choice Award, finalist
**Gryphon House / 16284 / Paperback**

# The Complete Daily Curriculum for Early Childhood
## Over 1200 Easy Activities to Support Multiple Intelligences and Learning Styles

*Pam Schiller and Pat Phipps*

Because there's more than one way to be smart! This innovative book for three- to six-year-olds offers a complete plan for every learning style. Organized by theme, *The Complete Daily Curriculum* includes a morning circle and end-of-day reflection, and different activities for each learning center. With over 1200 activities and ideas to engage multiple intelligences, plus assessment tools and a comprehensive appendix, you'll find everything you need to captivate and challenge every child in your classroom. 480 pages. 2002.
★ Early Childhood News Directors' Choice Award
**Gryphon House / 16279 / Paperback**